SHEET PAN

SCIENCE

THE
KITCHEN PANTRY
SCIENTIST

SHEET PAN
SCIENCE

25 Fun, Simple
Science Experiments
for the Kitchen Table

Super-Easy
Setup and
Cleanup

LIZ LEE HEINECKE
The Kitchen Pantry Scientist

QUARRY

Brimming with creative inspiration, how-to projects, and useful information to enrich your everyday life, quarto.com is a favorite destination for those pursuing their interests and passions.

First Published in 2022 by Quarry Books, an imprint of The Quarto Group,
100 Cummings Center, Suite 265-D, Beverly, MA 01915, USA.
T (978) 282-9590 F (978) 283-2742 Quarto.com

Quarry Books titles are also available at discount for retail, wholesale, promotional, and bulk purchase. For details, contact the Special Sales Manager by email at specialsales@quarto.com or by mail at The Quarto Group, Attn: Special Sales Manager,
100 Cummings Center, Suite 265-D, Beverly, MA 01915, USA.

10 9 8 7 6 5 4 3 2 1

ISBN: 978-0-7603-7567-9

Digital edition published in 2022
eISBN: 978-0-7603-7568-6

Library of Congress Cataloging-in-Publication Data is available.

Design and Page Layout: Laura Klynstra
Photography: Amber Procaccini Photography
Illustration of Liz Lee Heinecke: Mattie Wells

Printed in USA

THIS BOOK IS FOR EVERY

KID LIVING THROUGH THESE

CHALLENGING TIMES.

YOUR BRAVERY, HUMOR,

CREATIVITY, AND RESILIENCE

WILL TAKE YOU FAR.

WE ARE PROUD OF YOU.

CONTENTS

INTRODUCTION

Kids and science are a magical combination. Scientific exploration requires curiosity, and kids are famously curious. Most kids enjoy making a mess, and science can be wonderfully messy.

Enter the sheet pan, or rimmed baking sheet—a perfect vehicle for projects with a tendency to spill and overflow. With this simple metal tray, young learners can stir up loads of science fun while keeping drips and spills mostly contained.

Originally designed for professional kitchens, sheet pans have become a standard tool for the home cook. Often made of heavy aluminum to conduct heat evenly, the rimmed pans come in a variety of sizes. While full-sheet pans are designed to fit commercial ovens, half-sheet pans measure 18 by 13 inches (46 by 33 cm). You can even find sheet pans as small as an eighth of the size of a full sheet pan. Professional chefs nickname sheet pans by size—half-sheets, quarter-sheets, and eighth-sheets. Most home cooks use half-sheets, which are perfect for the projects in this book, but full sheets will work well too.

Sheet Pan Science contains twenty-five fun, educational projects that encourage kids to explore science concepts such as surface tension, germination, and capillary action using items many people have on hand. Each project in this book contains simple instructions, an easy-to-understand science explanation, and step-by-step photographic guides. Although a stovetop or freezer may occasionally be required, most steps of the experiments can be performed directly on a sheet pan, and each project is rated for messiness and complexity.

Messy play is important for young learners. Mixing colors, creating bubbly chemical reactions, and playing with goo are visual and tactile experiences that create strong memory pathways. In addition to allowing kids to explore and hone problem-solving skills, science experimentation encourages curiosity and engages a sense of wonder. A sheet pan and a few simple ingredients will instantly transform any kitchen countertop into a laboratory filled with scientific fun.

The projects in *Sheet Pan Science* cater to a wide range of interests. While some kids love getting their hands into cornstarch goo, others will enjoy creating colorful tie-dye milk. Using a lemon, aspiring geologists can test rock collections to see whether they contain limestone. Art-lovers may gravitate toward fabric-dyeing and leaf prints, while budding chefs can play with edible experiments.

So grab a sheet pan and a few simple ingredients and let the curiosity bubble over!

FIZZY SCIENCE

Bubbles, Rocks, and Ice Volcanoes

Around 2,500 years ago, the ancient Greeks invented the word "atom," which means "cannot be cut" or "indivisible." Today, we use the word "atom" to refer to the smallest pieces of stuff in our universe. Atoms are the building blocks of everything we can observe using the senses of sight, touch, taste, and smell. Chemical elements are pure substances made up of only one type of atom, such as carbon, silver, or helium.

A **chemical compound** is a combination of two or more chemical elements held together by invisible bonds. These bonds can be broken and new ones can form, depending on what other chemicals are close by. If you mix two or more chemicals together and the substances recombine and rearrange to make new chemical compounds, you've created what scientists call a **chemical reaction**.

In this chapter, you'll discover experiments that allow you to play with chemical compounds including baking soda, vinegar, citric acid, and detergent. The hands-on projects explore liquids, solids, and gases. You will also be able to experiment with chemical reactions that bubble and observe color changes as you learn about some chemical compounds you interact with every day.

LAB 1
ICE GLOBE VOLCANOES

MESS FACTOR *medium* | **COMPLEXITY** *low*

Mix up a bubbling chemical reaction inside hollow ice globes.

MATERIALS FIG. 1

Water
Balloons
Sheet pan
Scissors

¼ cup (55 g) baking soda for
    each globe
Food coloring of your choice
Jars or glasses

½ to 1 cup (120 to 240 ml)
    vinegar for each globe

SAFETY TIPS AND HINTS

★ Freeze several balloons at a time, if possible. In the freezer, air may not circulate evenly, and some ice globes may break when you remove the water.

★ In cold locations, balloons may be frozen outside when the temperature falls below freezing.

★ An adult may have to help chip a hole in the ice globe when it is removed from the freezer. It may take a few tries to get the ice thickness correct.

PROTOCOL

1. Use the tap in your kitchen sink to fill a balloon with water until it is 4 or 5 inches (10 or 12 cm) wide. Tie the end and place the balloon in a freezer. Fill more balloons and add them to the freezer as well. Try to position the balloons so that they aren't touching each other. **FIG. 2.**

2. Check the balloons periodically by tapping on the surface. When you feel a thick, solid shell of ice, remove one of the balloons from the freezer.

3. Place the balloon on a sheet pan or in a sink and use scissors to cut away the rubber.

4. Break through the weakest part of the ice to create a hole. An adult may have to help with this step if the ice is too thick to break easily.

5. Pour out the water in the middle of the globe. Check the ice for holes and return it to the freezer until you're ready to use it. **FIG. 3.**

6. If the ice froze evenly, you will have created a hollow globe that holds water without leaking. If it leaks, leave the balloons in the freezer for another hour or so before testing another one.

7. When you have some ice globes ready in the freezer, make "lava" solution by mixing 2 tablespoons (30 ml) water, ¼ cup baking soda, and several drops of food coloring together in a jar or glass. Make one jar of "lava" solution for each ice globe. **FIG. 4.**

8. Set small jars or glasses on a sheet pan to hold the ice globes. Position ice globes on the jars, hole-side up.

9. Fill each ice globe with "lava" solution. **FIG. 5.**

10. Add vinegar to a pouring vessel such as a liquid measuring cup.

11. Make the ice globe volcanoes erupt by pouring ½ to 1 cup (120 to 240 ml) vinegar into each globe. **FIG. 6.**

12. If there is lava solution left inside, pour more vinegar into the globes to create a second eruption of carbon dioxide bubbles. **FIG. 7.**

13. Try it again! Repeat the experiment using other colors. **FIG. 8.**

THE SCIENCE BEHIND THE FUN

Water in a balloon freezes from the outside in. The water nearest to the surface freezes first when the temperature drops to 32°F (0°C). This creates a shell of ice surrounding liquid water in the center. If you leave the balloon in the freezer for a long time, it will freeze into a solid globe.

Chemical reactions occur when two or more chemical compounds are combined and they make new chemicals. Often, it's easy to tell that chemical reactions are occurring because the reactions result in temperature change, color changes, smells, and bubbles. Inside a frozen globe, when baking soda combines with vinegar, a chemical reaction occurs. One of the products of the reaction is carbon dioxide gas—a gas spewed by real volcanoes. When enough gas pressure is produced, carbon dioxide bubbles are pushed up and out of the hole in the ice globes.

FIG. 1 Materials

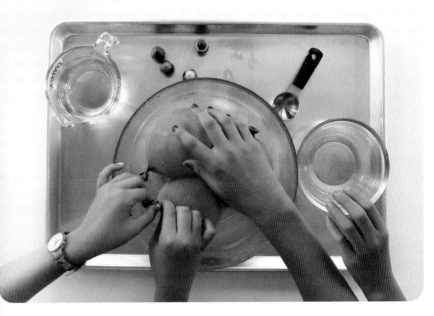

FIG. 2 Fill water balloons and freeze them until they are hollow globes.

FIG. 3 Peel the balloon off the ice globes and drain out water.

FIG. 4 Mix water, baking soda, and food coloring.

FIG. 5 Pour baking soda mixture into an ice globe.

FIG. 6 Add vinegar to the globe.

FIG. 7 Add more vinegar!

FIG. 8 Repeat the experiment using other colors.

LAB 2
MAGIC POTION

MESS FACTOR
medium

COMPLEXITY
low

Use red cabbage and water to create a pH-sensitive solution that changes color and makes a beautiful bubbly potion when combined with baking soda and vinegar.

MATERIALS FIG.1

½ head of red cabbage
Blender
Water

Containers such as cups or jars
Sheet pan
½ teaspoon (2 g) baking soda

¼ cup (60 ml) vinegar

SAFETY TIPS AND HINTS

Avoid splashing vinegar in your eyes. It will sting.

PROTOCOL

1. Chop up half a red cabbage and put it in a blender.

2. Cover the cabbage with water and blend. (If you don't have a blender, cook the cabbage and save the purple cooking water.) **FIG. 2.**

3. Strain out the liquid and save it. Discard the solids or cook something with them. Save the purple juice. **FIG. 3.**

4. Place two clear cups or jars on a sheet pan. Add around ¼ cup (60 ml) cabbage juice to each jar or cup. **FIG. 4.**

5. To one cup, add baking soda and stir. Observe the color change. **FIG. 5.**

6. To the other cup, add vinegar. **FIG. 6.**

7. Pour the pink vinegar solution into the blue baking soda solution to perform a chemical reaction that makes carbon dioxide gas. **FIG. 7.**

8. Feel the glass to see whether there was a temperature change from the chemical reaction. **FIG. 8.**

THE SCIENCE BEHIND THE FUN

Chemicals paint our world with color, and many living things contain brilliant chemical compounds. Red cabbage contains special substances called **anthocyanins (antho-sigh-an-ins)**, which can change color, depending on the environment.

The anthocyanins in red cabbage appear purple in water, which is neither an acid nor a base. However, if you add cabbage to a solution with a high pH, called a **base**, it turns blue or green. In an acidic solution with a low pH, called an **acid,** the compounds turn bright pink. Because of their pH sensitivity and this special color-changing property, anthocyanins are called **acid-base indicators**.

Objects appear to be one color or another because molecules in objects absorb certain wavelengths of light and reflect others. Anthocyanins change shape in different chemical environments. This causes them to absorb light differently, changing their appearance.

FIG. 1 Materials

FIG. 2 Blend red cabbage with water.

FIG. 3 Strain out the cabbage leaves.

FIG. 4 Pour cabbage juice into two cups or jars.

FIG. 5 Add baking soda to one of the cups.

FIG. 6 Add vinegar to the other cup.

FIG. 7 Pour the acidic pink solution into the basic blue solution.

FIG. 8 Observe the chemical reaction and check for temperature change.

LAB 3
GEOLOGY FIZZ TEST

MESS FACTOR
low

COMPLEXITY
low

Study rocks using a magnifying glass. Use lemon juice and vinegar to test whether the rocks contain any limestone.

MATERIALS FIG. I

A variety of rocks
Sheet pan
Magnifying glass
Penny
A lemon

Paper clip
Eyedropper
Magnets (optional)
Vinegar
Jars or glasses

Mineral identification book, website, or app (optional)
Notebook or note cards

SAFETY TIPS AND HINTS

The nasa.gov website contains great resources for learning more about rocks on Earth and on other planets.

PROTOCOL

1. Spread rocks out on a sheet pan. **FIG. 2.**

2. Think about where you found the rocks. Were there any geologic structures nearby, such as hills, bluffs, valleys, cliffs, rivers, or lakes? For example, most of the rocks in these photos were found on the shore of Lake Superior, and the limestone was found on a bluff in Kansas.

3. Observe each rock under a magnifying glass. **FIG. 3.**

4. Sort rocks into groups according to similar characteristics such as color, size, and surface texture.

5. Test rocks to see whether you can scratch them with a penny. **FIG. 4.**

6. Squeeze lemon juice into a small bowl.

7. Scratch the rocks with the sharp point of a paper clip to expose the minerals below the surface. **FIG. 5.**

8. Using an eyedropper, drip lemon juice on the scratches and use a magnifying glass to look for bubbles. If you see bubbles, the rock probably contains limestone. **FIG. 6.**

9. Test rocks with a magnet to see whether they contain magnetic material.

10. Place a rock containing limestone in a jar filled with vinegar to make the limestone dissolve. **FIG. 7**, **FIG. 8.**

11. Try to identify the rocks using a book, website, or app. Record your notes in a notebook or on a note card.

THE SCIENCE BEHIND THE FUN

Earth is an enormous ball of rock that is around four and a half billion years old. It is made up of four major parts: a solid inner core, a molten outer core, a rock mantle, and a thin outer crust that floats on the mantle. Mountains and valleys are formed when enormous segments of crust called **tectonic plates** collide or move apart. Most of the rocks lying around on the ground have been dug up or exposed by weather, water, and geologic activity. Layers of rocks can tell us things about the history of the Earth.

Minerals are specific chemical elements or chemical compounds found within rocks. They are the building blocks that make up our planet. Two minerals can be made up of similar chemicals but look very different. However, some minerals are harder than others, which can aid in identification. Rocks can be used to scratch each other to determine which is harder, or a copper penny can be used to see whether a rock is made of minerals harder than copper.

Limestone is a common rock composed of the minerals calcite and aragonite, which are crystalline forms of calcium carbonate. When citric acid or acetic acid (vinegar) is added to calcium carbonate, a chemical reaction occurs that dissolves the rock and creates carbon dioxide bubbles.

FIG. 1 Materials

FIG. 2 Spread rocks out on a sheet pan.

FIG. 3 Use a magnifying glass to study the rocks.

FIG. 4 Use a penny to test the hardness of different rocks.

FIG. 5 Scrape rocks with a metal paper clip and drip lemon juice onto the scraped area.

FIG. 6 Look for carbon dioxide bubbles, which indicate the presence of limestone.

FIG. 7 Place a rock containing limestone in vinegar.

FIG. 8 Bubbles will form as vinegar dissolves the limestone.

LAB 4
GEOMETRIC BUBBLES

MESS FACTOR	COMPLEXITY
medium	*medium*

Stir up a special bubble mix and make bubble wands that form pyramid- and cube-shaped bubbles.

MATERIALS FIG. I

Sheet pan
½ cup (64 g) cornstarch
6 cups (1.5 L) distilled or purified water
1 tablespoon (15 ml) glycerin (corn syrup may be substituted for glycerin)

1 tablespoon (14 g) baking powder
½ cup (120 ml) blue Dawn or Joy dish detergent (alternatively, use Dreft, Fairy, or Yes detergent)
Plastic straws
Pipe cleaners (chenille stems)

SAFETY TIPS AND HINTS

★ The detergents recommended in the materials list will give the best results.

★ Cut straws to even lengths for best results.

PROTOCOL

1. To contain the mess, place your measuring cup on a sheet pan. Mix cornstarch and water together. Add remaining ingredients. Stir gently and let the mixture sit while you construct bubble wands. **FIG. 2.**

2. Cut several plastic straws into short, even pieces, each 2 to 3 inches (5 to 7.5 cm) long. **FIG. 3.**

3. Make a pyramid wand. **FIG. 4.**

4. Put three short straws on a pipe cleaner. Leaving one end of the pipe cleaner sticking out a little bit, bend it into a triangle. Twist the short and long end of the pipe cleaner together to hold the triangle.

5. Twist a second pipe cleaner onto the long end of the first one. Add two more straws to the pipe cleaner and use them to make a second triangle.

6. Thread the pipe cleaner back through one of the straws.

7. Add one more straw to complete the pyramid and push the pipe cleaner through a second straw so that it comes out near the short piece of pipe cleaner. Twist the ends together so you have a handle for the bubble wand.

8. Submerge the wand in the bubble solution to experiment with the shape of bubbles made by a pyramid.

9. Use the same technique, starting with four short straws, to make a square and build a cubic bubble wand. Test the bubble shapes it creates. **FIG. 5.**

10. Take a normal-size straw, dip it in bubble solution, and blow bubbles inside the geometric bubbles. Try to make the bubbles expand beyond their usual geometry. **FIG. 6**, **FIG. 7.**

11. Try blowing bigger bubbles outdoors. **FIG. 8.**

THE SCIENCE BEHIND THE FUN

Water molecules like to stick together. Scientists call this attractive property **surface tension**, and it gives the surface of water an elastic quality. The detergent molecules in dish soap are called **surfactants**, and they have a hydrophilic (water-loving) end and a hydrophobic (water-hating) end. When you add detergent to water, it reduces the surface tension and allows bubbles to form easily.

The bubbles in this lab are pockets of air, trapped inside a thin film of water sandwiched between two layers of detergent. In bubble solution, chemicals such as glycerin and corn syrup slow down water layer evaporation, so bubbles last longer.

Normally, bubbles are round. In the air, they take on the form with the lowest surface area possible: a sphere. However, in this lab, the bubble mix sticks to the wands you constructed. Air is trapped inside when you remove the wand from the solution, and complicated three-dimensional bubbles form. Other factors, like your breath, can affect the shape of bubbles as well.

The thickness of the water/soap molecule is always changing slightly. As the water layer evaporates, light waves hit the soap layers from many angles, bounce around, and interfere with each other. That's why a rainbow of colors is visible in bubble film.

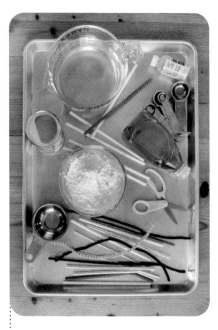

FIG. 1 Materials

FIG. 2 Mix up bubble solution.

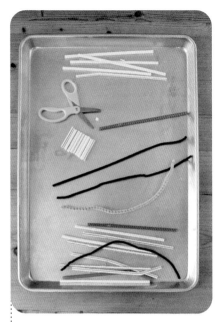

FIG. 3 Cut straws into equal lengths around 2 to 3 inches (5 to 7.5 cm) long.

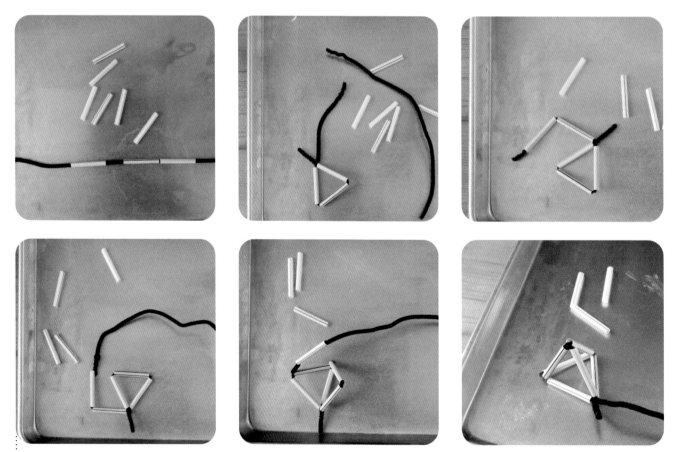

FIG. 4 Build a bubble wand. Add three straws to a pipe cleaner and bend into a triangle. Twist and add two more straws. Attach another pipe cleaner, form a second triangle, and then complete the pyramid using one more straw. Run the pipe cleaner back through the straws and twist to finish.

FIG. 5 Use the same wand-building technique to build a cubic wand, starting with a square.

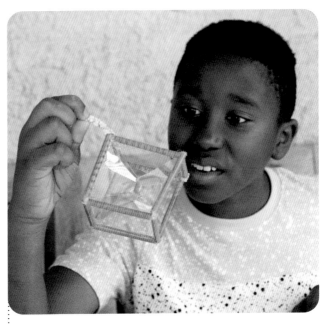

FIG. 6 Dip wands in bubble mix and observe the bubbles.

FIG. 7 Compare the triangular and cubic bubbles that form.

FIG. 8 Take the wands and bubble solution outdoors to blow larger bubbles.

LAB 5
FIZZY CANDY

Use citric acid and baking soda to make your favorite hard candy fizz.

MESS FACTOR
low

COMPLEXITY
low

MATERIALS FIG.1

Small bowls
¼ cup (30g) confectioners' sugar
1 teaspoon citric acid
    (available online and at
    most grocery stores)

½ teaspoon (2 g) baking soda
Water
Hard candy
Parchment paper or foil
Sheet pan

Pastry brush or cotton swab
2 plastic zipper bags

SAFETY TIPS AND HINTS

Hard candy is a choking hazard for young children.

PROTOCOL

1. In a small bowl, mix together confectioners' sugar, citric acid, and baking soda. **FIG. 2.**

2. Set the sugar mixture and a small bowl of water on a sheet pan.

3. Lay hard candy on parchment paper or foil on a sheet pan. **FIG. 3.**

4. Use a pastry brush or cotton swab to brush the candy with water so that it is damp but not soaking wet. **FIG. 4.**

5. Sprinkle both sides of the candy with the sugar mixture. **FIG. 5.**

6. Put some sugar mixture on your tongue to taste it. **FIG. 6**, **FIG. 7.**

7. When the candy is coated, store it in a candy bowl or a plastic zipper bag.

8. Measure 2 tablespoons (16 g) of the sugar mixture into another plastic zipper bag. Add ¼ cup (60 ml) water to see what happens when the mixture reacts with the saliva in your mouth. **FIG. 8.**

9. Note the temperature of the bag where the chemical reaction occurred. Does it feel warm or cold?

10. Create new mixtures of confectioners' sugar, citric acid, and baking soda using different ratios of the three ingredients to maximize flavor and fizziness. Test the mixtures in plastic zipper bags and on candy.

THE SCIENCE BEHIND THE FUN

The pieces of coated candy you make in this lab are chemical reactions waiting to happen. However, the sweet-sour treats won't fizz until you eat them. Water—the missing ingredient—is in your mouth. When the water in your saliva is added to citric acid and sodium bicarbonate (baking soda), a chemical reaction occurs. The acid reacts with the base (baking soda), and chemical bonds are rearranged. The products of this fizzy reaction are sodium citrate, water, and carbon dioxide gas bubbles, which you can feel on your tongue. Acids taste sour, which is why the citric acid-coated candy makes you pucker up.

When you do this reaction in a plastic bag, you'll notice that the water in the bag feels cold. That's because this chilly chemical reaction is called an **endothermic reaction**, which takes energy (heat) from the surrounding environment. **Exothermic reactions**, including combustion reactions such as fire, produce heat.

FIG. 1 Materials

FIG. 2 Mix confectioners' sugar, citric acid, and baking soda.

FIG. 3 Spread hard candy out on a piece of parchment paper or foil.

FIG. 4 Brush a light coating of water onto the candy.

FIG. 5 Dust the candy with a generous amount of sugar mixture.

FIG. 6 Put some sugar mixture on your tongue to taste it. Acids taste sour.

FIG. 7 The citric acid and baking soda will foam when they mix with saliva.

FIG. 8 Add a few tablespoons of sugar mixture to ¼ cup (60 ml) water and look for bubbles.

FLUID SCIENCE

Milk, Water, and Swirling Colors

A fluid is a substance such as a liquid or a gas whose molecules move easily past one another. Liquids have no fixed shape and can flow from one place to another. They easily change shape and will take the shape of the container that holds them. Because they do not offer much resistance to external stress, it's usually easy to stir fluids. Liquid water is a fluid that is very good at dissolving chemicals to form solutions. The number and type of atoms contained in a chemical solution determines its density.

Fluids containing water exhibit a physical property called **surface tension**, which describes the way water molecules on the surface of a liquid stick together to form a sort of "skin" on the top. This sticky property of water molecules also allows them to climb up narrow spaces, including those in paper, fabric, and plants, a phenomenon scientists call **capillary action**. Soaps and detergents can be used to break the surface tension of a fluid.

In this unit, you will see the forces of physics in action when you make marker tie-dye and create a walking rainbow. Spectacular swirling food coloring illustrates how detergent can break the surface tension of milk, and you can create a colorful cabbage using capillary action. Artists will especially enjoy floating paint on a seaweed substance to fabricate photo-worthy marbled paper.

LAB 6
WALKING RAINBOW

MESS FACTOR *medium* | COMPLEXITY *low*

Watch capillary action fill jars with a rainbow of colors.

MATERIALS FIG.1

Paper towels
Water

7 jars or glasses of approximately
    equal size
Sheet pan

Red, blue, and yellow food
    coloring

SAFETY TIPS AND HINTS

For the best results, paper towels should be cut to the same length after folding to ensure they just reach the bottom of two jars. See photographs on page 36.

PROTOCOL

1. Cut, fold, and trim six paper towels into *V*-shaped "wicks" that are long enough to reach from the bottom of one jar to the bottom of the next jar without sticking up into the air. Ideally, each wick will be folded over twice and will barely rest on the rims of the jars. **FIG. 2.**

2. Line seven jars up on a sheet pan. Fill one of the end jars and then every other jar with water. **FIG. 3.**

3. Add several drops of red food coloring to each of the water-filled jars on the ends. Add blue food coloring to one of the other water-filled jars and yellow food coloring to the final water-filled jar. **FIG. 4.**

4. Stir the food coloring into the water. **FIG. 5.**

5. Make paper towel bridges between each of the jars so that the ends of the folded towels sit evenly in each jar. **FIG. 6.**

6. Watch as the water begins to move up the paper wicks via capillary action. **FIG. 7.**

7. Try to predict what colors will be created in the empty glasses. **FIG. 8.**

8. Leave the jars alone until they have all filled to the same level with liquid. Observe the colors created by the mixing of primary colors red, yellow, and blue.

THE SCIENCE BEHIND THE FUN

In this lab, a physical force called **capillary action** pulls water through narrow spaces between the fibers in paper, which act as microscopic siphons. Another force, called **surface tension**, helps the water molecules stick together as they move. Colorful food dyes move with the water and mix with the dye in the next glass to form new colors. Once equal amounts of water have filled each of the glasses, the water will stop flowing, and you will be able to study the colors you created by mixing red, yellow, and blue.

The colors we see with our eyes are produced in our brains by light-sensing cells called **cones**. These specialized cells detect electromagnetic radiation (light), which travels in waves. The longest light waves human eyes can detect are red. Green light waves are somewhere in the middle, and violet waves are the shortest ones we can see. Colors are made up of mixtures of red, green, and violet light waves.

FIG. 1 Materials

FIG. 2 Fold paper towels into long strips.

FIG. 3 Line up seven jars and fill every other jar with water.

FIG. 4 Add red food coloring to jars on each end and yellow and blue to the other two jars.

FIG. 5 Stir food coloring into the water.

FIG. 6 Make the paper towels into bridges between the jars with their ends in the colorful water.

FIG. 7 Watch as the water moves through the paper towels via capillary action.

FIG. 8 Observe the color mixing that occurs.

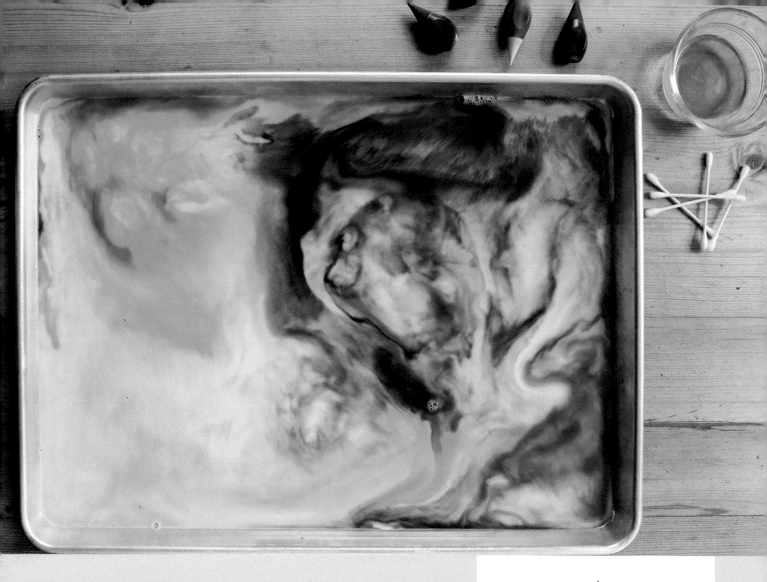

LAB 7
TIE-DYE MILK

Learn about surface tension by creating swirling, colorful patterns in milk.

MESS FACTOR	COMPLEXITY
medium	*low*

MATERIALS FIG. 1

About 4 cups (1 L) milk
Sheet pan
3 teaspoons (15 ml) water

1 teaspoon (5 ml) dishwashing
   detergent or liquid hand soap
Small dish

Multiple colors of food coloring
Cotton swab

SAFETY TIPS AND HINTS

✱ Food coloring stains, so wear old clothes to try this experiment.

✱ If you don't want to use so much milk, set a plate on the sheet pan and perform the experiment on the plate.

PROTOCOL

1. Pour milk onto a sheet pan or a plate to form a thin layer. **FIG. 2.**

2. Mix together water and dishwashing detergent or liquid hand soap in a small dish. **FIG. 3.**

3. Add several drops of food coloring to the milk on the pan. Use multiple colors and space the drops out. **FIG. 4.**

4. Dip a cotton swab into the dish detergent solution. **FIG. 5.**

5. Carefully, touch the wet swab to the milk. Try not to stir it around. The detergent will break the surface tension of the milk, allowing the food coloring to swirl around in beautiful patterns. **FIG. 6**, **FIG. 7.**

6. You can keep rewetting your cotton swab with soapy water and touching it to the milk. Touch the swab to the bottom of the plate and hold it there for a few seconds. **FIG. 8.**

7. Take a photo of your colorful science project.

THE SCIENCE BEHIND THE FUN

If you've ever tested how many drops of water you can add to the top of a penny, you have seen the forces of surface tension at work. Water molecules stick together and form a bulging droplet on the penny before bursting and running over the edge. This happens because the surface of liquids is similar to a stretched elastic skin, like the rubber on a balloon full of air. Surface tension is the scientific name for the way the "skin" of a liquid sticks together.

In this experiment, you pour milk, which is mostly made of water, onto a sheet pan, forming a large liquid surface. Food coloring is also made of water mixed with lots of colorful chemicals called **pigments**. This weighs the food coloring down and keeps it from mixing with the milk quickly so that when you add drops of food coloring to the milk, they stay in one spot for a while.

Dish detergent is like a chemical knife that breaks the "skin" of the milk, like a pin popping a balloon. When the surface tension is broken, food coloring and milk escape from beneath the milk's surface, swirling to the top where they mix together.

FIG. 1 Materials

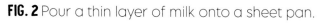
FIG. 2 Pour a thin layer of milk onto a sheet pan.

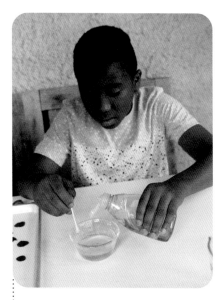
FIG. 3 Mix dish detergent and water together in a small bowl.

FIG. 4 Drip liquid food coloring into the milk.

FIG. 5 Dip a cotton swab in the detergent/water mixture and touch it to the surface of the milk without stirring.

FIG. 6 The dish detergent is a chemical called a surfactant that can break the surface tension of the milk.

FIG. 7 When the surface tension is broken, food coloring swirls around to create beautiful patterns.

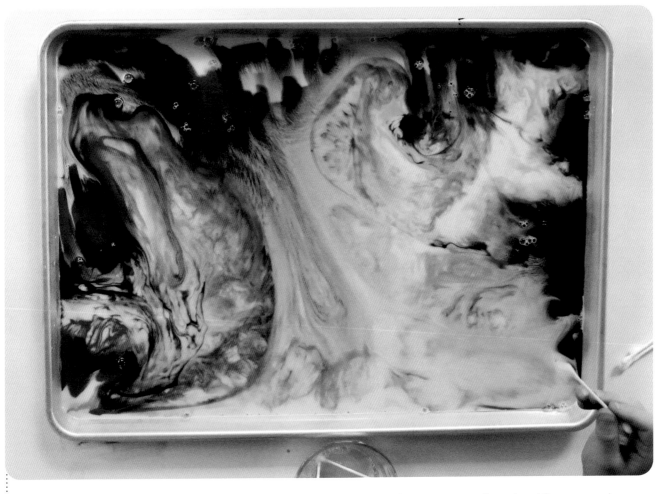

FIG. 8 Touch more soap to the surface and then leave the sheet pan undisturbed for several minutes to see what happens to the colors.

LAB 8
MARKER MAGIC

Use permanent markers and rubbing alcohol to make colorful designs that mimic tie-dye.

MESS FACTOR *low* | **COMPLEXITY** *low*

MATERIALS FIG. 1

Cloth items to decorate (cotton T-shirts, socks, dish towels, or shoelaces)

Plastic cups or glass jars

Rubber bands

Colorful permanent markers (such as Sharpies)

Rubbing alcohol (isopropyl alcohol)

Sheet pan

Eyedropper or small syringe

SAFETY TIPS AND HINTS

Rubbing alcohol is poisonous if swallowed, so parental supervision is required for this project. Do this experiment outdoors or in a well-ventilated area. Do not expose fabric containing alcohol to heat until it is completely dry because rubbing alcohol and its fumes are flammable.

PROTOCOL

1. Stretch a T-shirt or other cloth item over the mouth of a cup or jar and secure it with rubber bands. Set the jar on a sheet pan. **FIG. 2.**

2. Use permanent markers to make several dime-sized dots of different colors on the stretched cotton. **FIG. 3.**

3. Set a bottle of rubbing alcohol on the sheet pan. Label alcohol with a poison symbol so it is not mistaken for water. Fill an eyedropper or syringe with alcohol and drip it onto the spots of color until the alcohol starts to soak outward, carrying the ink with it. The pan will catch any stray drips. **FIG. 4.**

4. Repeat steps 1 to 3 on different areas of the item, decorating until the design is complete. **FIG. 5, FIG 6, FIG. 7.**

5. Allow the dyed cotton to dry overnight. When completely dry, hang it in the sun for a few hours or put it in the dryer for 15 minutes to set the color. Wash marker tie-dye separately from other clothes. **FIG. 8.**

THE SCIENCE BEHIND THE FUN

Permanent marker ink doesn't dissolve in water. However, special chemicals called **solvents** can break it down. Rubbing alcohol is one of these solvents. When you drip it on the cloth, it dissolves the colorful ink and carries it through the fabric.

Some ink colors are made up of smaller chemical compounds than other colors. Small chemicals move through the fabric more quickly and spread out faster than larger compounds, and inks containing more than one color separate out into multiple hues. The alcohol eventually evaporates into the air, leaving ink designs behind in the fabric.

FIG. 1 Materials

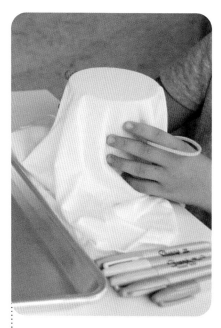

FIG. 2 Use a rubber band to secure fabric onto a cup or jar.

FIG. 3 Draw large dots of color on the fabric with permanent marker.

FIG. 4 Drip rubbing alcohol (isopropyl alcohol) onto each dot.

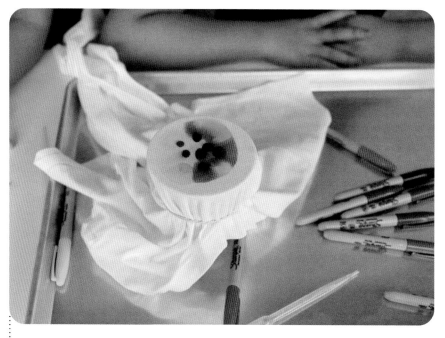

FIG. 5 Observe the ink as it spreads out with the alcohol, which is a chemical called a solvent.

FIG. 6 You can do the same thing with white shoelaces, if you have some on hand.

FIG. 7 Perform this lab in a well-ventilated area and supervise small children. Rubbing alcohol is poisonous, if consumed.

FIG. 8 Once it is dry, fabric containing permanent marker will retain its color when washed.

LAB 9
MARBLED PAPER

Float paint on thickened water to create beautiful designs that can be transferred to paper treated with alum.

MESS FACTOR *high*	**COMPLEXITY** *medium*

MATERIALS FIG. I

1.9 oz (53 g) alum (aluminum sulfate), available online and in the spice section of grocery stores

About 22 cups (5.5 L) water

Paintbrush and/or eyedropper

Heavy-weight white craft paper or watercolor paper

Pencil

Blender

2 tablespoons (256 g) carrageenan (marbling size), available online (corn starch may be substituted; see "Safety Tips and Hints")

Liquid acrylic paint (several colors)

Toothpicks

Baking rack (optional)

SAFETY TIPS AND HINTS

✱ Paper and carrageenan-thickened water should be prepared the day before you do this lab. See "Protocol."

✱ Carrageenan works better than cornstarch as a water thickener, but cornstarch is a decent substitute and doesn't have to sit overnight. To use cornstarch instead of carrageenan, dissolve 4 tablespoons (32 g) cornstarch in ½ cup (120 ml) cold water. Bring 6 cups (1.5 L) water to a boil in a saucepan. Add the cornstarch solution to the water, stir well, and boil for 1 minute. Turn the heat to low and simmer for 2 more minutes, stirring occasionally. Cool and thin to the consistency of heavy cream by adding water.

PROTOCOL

1. Mix alum into 6 cups (1.5 L) water. Note: Alum solution may be saved and used in Lab 21 for fabric dyeing.

2. Sponge or brush the solution onto several pieces of heavy paper, such as watercolor paper, and lightly mark the side you treated with a pencil. Alternately, dip the paper in the alum solution. Allow the paper to dry completely. **FIG. 2.**

3. In a blender, blend 1 tablespoon (128 g) carrageenan into ½ gallon (2 L) water for 30 seconds. Pour into a container for storage. Combine another tablespoon (128 g) carrageenan with ½ gallon (2 L) of water and mix again. Combine the two batches and let them sit overnight. (They'll keep for about 2 days.)

4. When you are ready to marble, pour a thin layer of carrageenan (or cornstarch) solution onto a sheet pan. **FIG. 3.**

5. Add some water to acrylic paint and mix until it is the consistency of whole milk. **FIG. 4.**

6. Drip or use a brush to spatter the thinned liquid acrylic paint into the water. Cover the entire surface with paint. **FIG. 5.**

7. Use toothpicks to make marbled patterns. **FIG. 6.**

8. When your design is complete, carefully place a piece of paper on the paint, alum-side down, and smooth it gently to remove bubbles. **FIG. 7.**

9. Carefully lift the paper out of the paint. Drag it against the edge of the pan to remove excess paint, if you wish. **FIG. 8.**

10. Briefly rinse the colorful paper in the sink to wash off extra paint so that you can see the design more clearly.

11. Dry the paper on a baking rack or sheet pan.

THE SCIENCE BEHIND THE FUN

Alum is a useful type of chemical called a **mordant**. Mordants are good at combining with other chemicals, making them get stuck so they can't move around. Alum is often used in dyeing cloth (see Lab 21), but mordants can be used to help stain other things, including bacteria. In this project, alum on the paper combines with paint to make it stick.

Carrageenans are large, long chainlike molecules made by edible red seaweeds. Their size and flexibility allow them to form gel-like substances. At the grocery store, you might find carrageenans in dairy products, like yogurt, where they are used as a thickener. In this lab, we use them to thicken water so that paint will float on top of it.

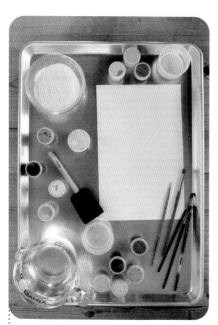

FIG. 1 Materials

FIG. 2 Brush or sponge alum solution onto the paper. Dry.

FIG. 3 Pour carrageenan- or cornstarch-thickened water onto a sheet pan.

FIG. 4 Use water to thin acrylic paint.

FIG. 5 Drip and splatter paint onto the thickened water in the sheet pan.

FIG. 6 Use a toothpick to create designs in the paint.

FIG. 7 Lay a piece of paper, alum-side down, on the paint.

FIG. 8 Lift the paper carefully and rinse in the sink. Try not to leave fingerprints on the front of the paper. Set it on a baking rack or sheet pan to dry.

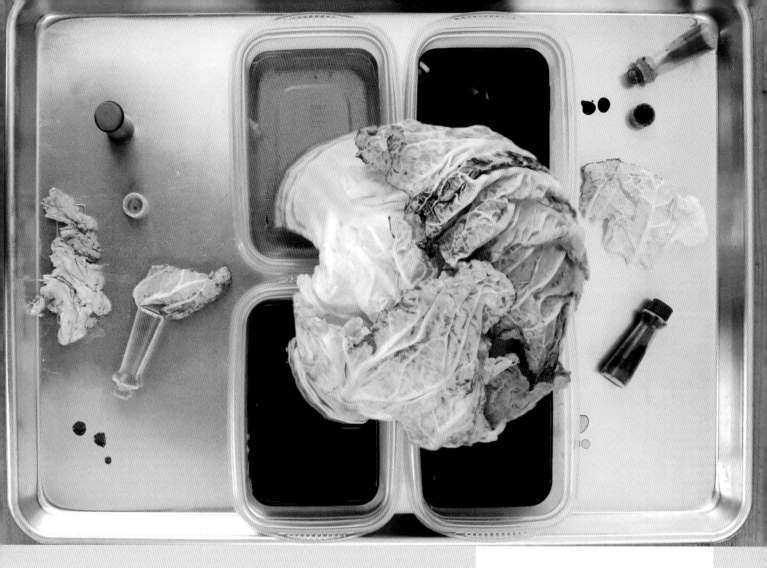

LAB 10
COLORFUL CABBAGE

MESS FACTOR
medium

COMPLEXITY
low

Observe capillary action in motion by transforming a cabbage into a rainbow of color.

MATERIALS FIG.1

Head of Napa cabbage

4 containers of equal size, large enough to hold the bottom of a Napa cabbage

Warm water

Blue, red, yellow, and green food coloring

Sheet pan

Knife

Rubber bands

SAFETY TIPS AND HINTS

An adult should help cut the cabbage.

PROTOCOL

1. Remove any loose leaves from a head of the Napa cabbage. **FIG. 2.**

2. Fill four containers three-quarters full with warm (not hot) water. **FIG. 3.**

3. Add ten or more drops of blue food coloring to the first container, ten or more drops of red food coloring to the second container, ten or more drops of yellow food coloring to the third container, and ten or more drops of green food coloring to the fourth container. **FIG. 4.**

4. Arrange the containers of colorful water in a tight formation in the center of a sheet pan.

5. Using a sharp knife, cut the cabbage in half vertically, from the bottom up, leaving the top 4 inches (10 cm) or so intact so that cabbage is still together at the crown. If possible, try to cut down the middle of large leaves. Rotate the cabbage and repeat so that the bottom section is cut into four parts. **FIG. 5.**

6. Use rubber bands to secure the bottoms of each quarter of the cabbage. **FIG. 6.**

7. Make a fresh cut at the bottom of the cabbage, a few inches up from the old cut.

8. Place each quarter of the cabbage in a container of water so that one is in red, one is in blue, one is in yellow, and one is in green.

9. Check the cabbages every hour or so to observe how the food coloring is moving up into the leaves. Leave the cabbage in the colored water overnight. **FIG. 7.**

10. Study the leaves closely to see where the dye traveled. **FIG. 8.**

THE SCIENCE BEHIND THE FUN

Water molecules are simple chemicals made up of two hydrogen atoms and one oxygen atom. Strongly attracted to each other, water molecules tend to stick together. In a narrow tube made of a surface that attracts water, the attraction between the surface and water, coupled with the attraction of the water molecules to each other, pulls water up through the tube.

Scientists call this type of movement capillary action, and the forces involved are strong enough to defy gravity. Plants are composed of huge numbers of tube-shaped cells that take advantage of these physical forces, and the specialized tissue made up of these long, narrow tubes can carry water from the ground to a tree's highest branches. In this experiment, colored water is taken up via capillary action into a cabbage.

FIG. 1 Materials

FIG. 2 Remove any loose leaves from the cabbage.

FIG. 3 Fill four containers with water.

FIG. 4 Add food coloring to each container: red, blue, yellow, and green.

FIG. 5 Cut the base of the cabbage into four equal sections, leaving the leaves above the cuts intact.

FIG. 6 Secure each section with a rubber band, make a fresh cut at the bottom, and place each section in a different color.

FIG. 7 Let the cabbage sit for 24 hours. Check it every few hours to see what is happening.

FIG. 8 Remove the cabbage from the water and observe the paths of the food coloring.

EDIBLE SCIENCE

Marshmallows, Sugar Crystals, and Acid Dyes

Physics, biology, and chemistry come into play every time food is prepared. Cooking pasta requires heating water until it is hot enough to turn into a gas, forming bubbles inside the liquid. Acids such as vinegar and lemon juice enhance flavors. Wheat flour contains a protein called **gluten** that combines with water to form long, chewy strands. Crystals form the foundation of ice cream.

In this unit, you will experiment with food science using ingredients you may already have on hand, such as food coloring, which is an acid dye. Use yeast to inflate plastic bags with carbon dioxide gas and make delicious dinner rolls. Mush marshmallows, which contain a colloid called **gelatin**, into a tasty goo to create a flexible cake decoration called **fondant**. You'll learn to grow sugar crystals that look like tiny gems and dehydrate fruit to make tasty fruit roll-ups. The results will be delicious.

LAB 11

MARSHMALLOW MUSH FONDANT

MESS FACTOR *high*	**COMPLEXITY** *low*

Use marshmallows to make a gelatinous goo that can be transformed into an edible playdough called fondant.

MATERIALS FIG. 1

½ ounce (14g) good white baking chocolate containing cocoa butter

3 cups (180 g) small marshmallows

1 tablespoon (14 g) butter, cut up

1½ (7 ml) teaspoons milk

Microwaveable bowl

Microwave

1 teaspoon (5 ml) clear vanilla extract

1½ cups (180 g) confectioners' sugar, plus more for kneading

Spatula or rubber scraper

Sheet pan

Food coloring of your choice

Rolling pin

Small cookie cutters/fondant molds (optional)

SAFETY TIPS AND HINTS

✶ The marshmallow mixture is very sticky at first, but it will get less and less sticky as confectioners' sugar is kneaded in.

✶ To cover a cake or cupcake with fondant, frost it first to create a smooth base.

PROTOCOL

1. Chop chocolate into small pieces. Combine chopped white chocolate, marshmallows, butter, and milk in a microwavable bowl. **FIG. 2.**

2. Microwave on high for 1 minute and stir until smooth. If needed, microwave for 30 seconds as needed until everything is melted. **FIG. 3.**

3. Stir in clear vanilla extract and mix.

4. Add confectioners' sugar and stir to combine.

5. Sprinkle a sheet pan with confectioners' sugar and scrape the marshmallow mixture onto the sugar-coated surface. **FIG. 4.**

6. Dust the marshmallow mix with more confectioners' sugar and knead it on the pan, incorporating confectioners' sugar until it is no longer sticky. You may need to add more confectioners' sugar. It will probably take 5 to 10 minutes of kneading, and you may have to occasionally scrape the mixture off your fingers with a spatula or rubber scraper. **FIG. 5.**

7. Use food coloring to tint the fondant by kneading the color in. Make it all one color or divide it and create several colors. **FIG. 6.**

8. Fondant dries out quickly, so use a rolling pin to roll it out and then wrap it in plastic until you're ready to use it. Fondant can be stored for a week or two at room temperature, tightly wrapped.

9. Use cookie cutters or your hands to cut and shape the fondant into decorations to top a cake or cupcakes. Fondant can also be used to make sugar crystal geodes, like the ones in Lab 12, but you will want to quadruple the recipe. **FIG. 7.**

THE SCIENCE BEHIND THE FUN

Gelatin is a protein that can be dissolved in hot water and cooled to form a gel. Scientists call gels like these, where liquids are trapped in solids, **colloids**. Gelatin plays an important role in many foods, including marshmallows and fondant.

Soft, chewy candies like marshmallows are made by beating hot sugar syrup with gelatin and water to make air bubbles in the mixture. As the foam cools, air bubbles are trapped inside as the gelatin turns from a liquid into a gel. Along with gelatin, corn syrup helps prevent sugar in the marshmallows from crystallizing, keeping marshmallows (and fondant) soft and chewy.

FIG. 1 Materials

FIG. 2 Add marshmallows, milk, butter, and white chocolate to a microwaveable bowl.

FIG. 3 Microwave briefly and mix well.

FIG. 4 Stir in confectioners' sugar and pour onto sugar-coated sheet pan.

FIG. 5 Wash hands and knead the mixture, adding confectioners' sugar until it is no longer sticky.

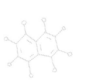

FIG. 6 Form the fondant into balls and add food coloring.

FIG. 7 Roll, cut, and sculpt the fondant.

LAB 12
SUGAR CRYSTAL GEODES

Grow sparkling sugar crystals in a fondant shell using supersaturated sugar solution.

MATERIALS FIG. 1

3 cups (600 g) granulated sugar
About 1 cup (237 ml) water
Medium saucepan
Food coloring of your choice
Nonstick baking paper such as parchment or waxed paper
Sheet pan
Fondant (see Lab 11 to make your own)
Rolling pin
Aluminum foil
Small to medium bowl
Cooking spray or oil (optional)
Magnifying glass

MESS FACTOR	COMPLEXITY
medium	*medium*

SAFETY TIPS AND HINTS

Adult supervision recommended while making hot sugar syrup. Once syrup has cooled to room temperature, kids can take over.

PROTOCOL

1. Combine granulated sugar with water in a medium saucepan. Bring ingredients to a boil until all the sugar is dissolved and the syrup is clear. **FIG. 2.**

2. Add food coloring to the syrup to create the color you want the crystals to appear.

3. Allow the syrup to cool to a safe temperature while you make the outside of the geode.

4. Lay down a sheet of nonstick baking paper on a flat surface such as a full-sheet pan or a tabletop. (If rolling on a sheet pan, you may have to put a silicon potholder under the pan to keep it from sliding around.)

5. Mix white, black, and other fondant colors together in clumps and form them into a ball. Twist the fondant and fold it once or twice slightly so that the colors are combined but not completely mixed. Roll the fondant into a circle large enough to cover the outside of the bowl you will use for the geode. **FIG. 3, FIG. 4, FIG. 5.**

6. Roll out a second piece of white fondant approximately the same size as the first one.

7. Rub a small amount of water across the colorful fondant to moisten the surface and make it sticky. Flip the white fondant over and lay it across the colorful fondant so that they stick together. Remove the baking paper from the top of the white fondant. **FIG. 6.**

8. Completely cover a large sheet pan with foil. Fold two sheets of foil together if necessary.

9. Place a folded kitchen towel in the center of the foil and place a bowl on top of the towel.

10. Place another piece of foil on top of the bowl and push it to the bottom, forming it to the bowl so that it forms a crumpled surface inside the bowl.

11. Add a second piece of foil to emphasize the crumpled surface, which will form the surface of the geode. **FIG. 7.**

12. Spray the foil inside the bowl with cooking spray or oil it lightly. **FIG. 8.**

13. Flip the fondant over and lay it across the foil-lined bowl, white fondant up.

14. Remove the baking paper and press the fondant into the bowl. **FIG. 9.**

15. Press a few sugar crystals into the fondant and then fill the fondant bowl to the top with sugar syrup. **FIG. 10.**

16. Pull the foil lining on the sheet pan up around the bowl to form a protective cover. Set the sheet pan somewhere where it will not be disturbed for several days. **FIG. 11.**

17. Open the foil case and pour the excess syrup into a container. Observe the crystals. **FIG. 12.**

18. Break off any crystals you don't like.

19. Remove the towel from the sheet pan. Add another piece of foil and turn the bowl upside down to dry. **FIG. 13.**

20. Trim off any excess fondant and observe the sugar crystals through a magnifying glass. **FIG. 14, FIG. 15.**

21. Allow the geodes to dry, crystal-side down. When they are dry, turn them over to reveal the sparkling crystals inside. **FIG. 16.**

THE SCIENCE BEHIND THE FUN

Crystals such as sugar crystals are solids formed by a network of repeating chemical building blocks, like bricks in a wall. The crystals formed by sucrose (table sugar) are six-sided prisms. Crystals that share the same chemical makeup can be big or small, but they are always the same shape.

To make large sugar crystals for fondant geodes, you cook up sugar syrup, which scientists call a **supersaturated sugar solution**. Heating the water and sugar together allows the water to hold more sugar molecules that it normally would at room temperature. Crystals form when the syrup encounters a "seed molecule" such as the sugar crystals in the fondant, and molecules from the sugar start snapping together into a solid crystal structure.

FIG. 1 Materials

FIG. 2 Make a sugar syrup.

FIG. 3 Combine black, white, and colorful fondant into a ball.

FIG. 4 Roll out the fondant.

FIG. 5 The fondant slab should be large enough to cover the outside of your bowl.

FIG. 6 Roll a piece of white fondant the same size and lay it over the colorful fondant slab.

FIG. 7 Cover the inside of a bowl with two layers of aluminum foil.

FIG. 8 Lightly oil the foil so the fondant won't stick.

FIG. 9 Put the fondant into the bowl, white-side up, and mold it to the foil lining.

FIG. 10 After pressing a few sugar crystals into the fondant, fill the bowl with sugar syrup.

FIG. 11 Cover the bowl with foil and let it sit undisturbed for 5 to 7 days.

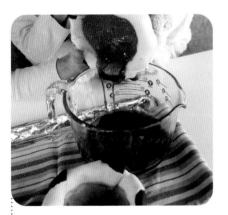

FIG. 12 Pour the syrup out of the fondant-lined bowl. You may have to break a layer of crystals on the surface of the liquid.

FIG. 13 Turn the bowls upside down on a sheet pan to drain.

FIG. 14 Trim off excess fondant to create the edge of your geode.

FIG. 15 Study the shape of the sugar crystals.

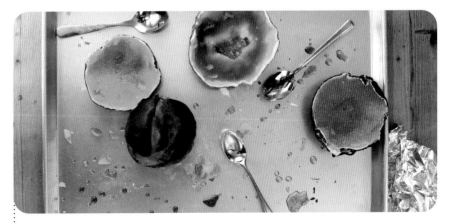

FIG. 16 Allow the geodes to dry, crystal-side down. When they are dry, turn them over to reveal the sparkling crystals inside.

LAB 13
DYNAMITE FRUIT ROLL-UPS

Learn about dehydration and food preservation by making delicious fruit snacks.

MATERIALS FIG. 1

Oven

6 cups (720 g) fresh or frozen fruit, chopped

¾ cup (177 ml) water (optional)

1 tablespoon (15 ml) lemon juice

8 tablespoons (160 g) honey if using strawberries or blueberries, 4 tablespoons (80 g) if using mangoes or peaches

Large saucepan

Food processor, blender, or hand blender (optional)

Fork

Silicon baking mat (or parchment paper)

Sheet pan

SAFETY TIPS AND HINTS

✱ Hot fruit leather can cause burns. An adult should supervise cooking. Allow the fruit leather to cool before tasting it. It will take several hours to bake.

✱ Silicon mats work better than parchment paper for drying fruit leather, but you can use either.

✱ Frozen mango dries quickly and makes delicious fruit roll-ups. Berries make good fruit leather but are stickier.

PROTOCOL

1. Preheat the oven to lowest setting (170°F, or 77°C).

2. Add chopped fruit to a saucepan. If using mango, add ¾ cup (177 ml) water to the mixture.

3. Stir in lemon juice and some honey to the fruit. Blueberries and strawberries require more honey (8 tablespoons [160 g]) than mango or peaches (4 tablespoons [80 g]). **FIG. 2.**

4. Cook fruit mixture over medium heat, stirring occasionally until it has a soft, jamlike consistency and most of the water has evaporated. **FIG. 3.**

5. Cool fruit mixture completely.

6. Mash the cooked fruit with a fork, or blend it using a blender, food processor, hand blender, until it is smooth. **FIG. 4.**

7. Spread the fruit into a thin, even layer on a silicone mat (or parchment paper) on a sheet pan. **FIG. 5.**

8. Bake the fruit for several hours, until it is no longer sticky. It may get a little bit crisp at the edges. **FIG. 6.**

9. Cool the dried fruit, peel it off the baking mat or parchment paper, and cut off the crispy edges. **FIG. 7.**

10. Roll the fruit leather up, cut it into small rolls if desired, and store it in parchment paper or a plastic bag until you eat it. **FIG. 8.**

THE SCIENCE BEHIND THE FUN

Microbes such as bacteria and fungi cover every surface you can see, including food. Heating food up, refrigerating and freezing it, and exposing it to concentrated chemicals like sugar and salt are some methods of killing microbes or slowing their growth.

Desiccation (drying) is one of the oldest methods of keeping food delicious and safe to eat. Although drying doesn't kill all the microbes found on food, limiting water is a good way to stop them from growing so they can't produce toxins that can make people sick. High salt and sugar concentrations also kill bacteria. Fruit leather and other dried fruit contain quite a bit of sugar and can be kept for up to a week outside the fridge.

FIG. I Materials

FIG. 2 Add fruit, water, and honey to a saucepan.

FIG. 3 Cook the fruit until it has a jamlike consistency.

FIG. 4 Blend the fruit until smooth and pour it onto a baking mat or parchment paper.

FIG. 5 Spread the puree evenly onto a baking mat.

FIG. 6 Bake at a low temperature until the fruit is no longer sticky.

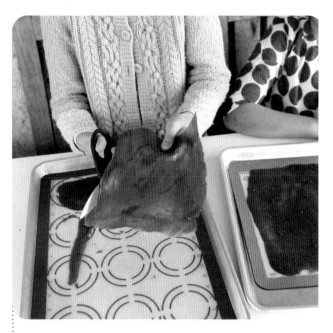

FIG. 7 Peel the fruit off the sheet pan and cut off any dry edges.

FIG. 8 Roll up the dried fruit and taste your healthy, homemade snack.

LAB 14
YEASTY BEASTS

Make tasty dinner rolls to see how yeast are living organisms that make bubbles as they grow.

MATERIALS FIG. 1

Large mixing bowl
Sheet pan
6 tablespoons (85 g) softened butter, plus more for optional
    greasing
2 tablespoons (26 g) granulated sugar, plus 2 teaspoons (9 g) for
    yeast experiment
1 teaspoon (6 g) salt
Fork
2 eggs (and an extra egg if you want to do an egg wash)
1 cup (237 ml) milk
Microwavable bowl or saucepan
4 cups (500 g) flour, plus more for kneading
4½ teaspoons (18 g) active dry yeast
Plastic wrap or a damp towel
Oven
½ cup (120 ml) water
Plastic zipper bag
Parchment paper (optional)
Kitchen shears or clean scissors (optional)
Dried fruit, such as raisins or cranberries (optional)

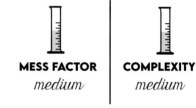

MESS FACTOR	COMPLEXITY
medium	*medium*

SAFETY TIPS AND HINTS

An adult should supervise taking hot rolls out of the oven.

PROTOCOL

1. Set a large mixing bowl on a sheet pan. Add the softened butter, 2 tablespoons (26 g) sugar, and salt to the bowl and mix well with a fork. **FIG. 2.**

2. Crack two eggs and add them to the mixture. Beat the eggs with a fork and mix them in with the butter, sugar, and salt as well as you can. The mixture will be chunky. **FIG. 3.**

3. Warm the milk in a microwavable container or in a pan so that it feels warm but not hot. (Thirty seconds in a microwave usually works well.) Stir it into the mixture in the bowl and mix until somewhat smooth. **FIG. 4.**

4. Add flour onto the top of the liquid in the bowl. Before mixing, add 2¼ teaspoons (9 g) yeast to the flour and stir together with a fork. Mix yeast and flour into the liquid until it forms a large, shaggy ball of dough. **FIG. 5, FIG. 6.**

5. Sprinkle flour on the sheet pan and dump the bread dough onto the flour. Knead the dough for about 5 minutes by gathering it together and pushing on it with the palms of both hands. Fold it over, rotate it, and repeat. If it gets too sticky, sprinkle flour on the sheet pan and the dough and continue kneading. **FIG. 7**, **FIG. 8.**

6. Put the dough back in the bowl, cover with plastic wrap or a damp towel, and let it rise for about 45 minutes. **FIG. 9.**

7. Preheat the oven to 375°F (190°C, or gas mark 5). While the dough rises, do an experiment to see how growing yeast makes carbon dioxide. On the sheet pan, add 2¼ teaspoons (9 g) yeast, 2 teaspoons (9 g) sugar, and water to a plastic zipper bag. Squeeze the air out of the bag and seal it. **FIG. 10**, **FIG. 11.**

8. Wash the sheet pan and set the bowl of dough and yeast-filled plastic bag side by side on the pan to observe how they change as the yeasts grow and produce gas bubbles.

9. After 45 minutes, remove the plastic from the dough and punch it once to release some of the carbon dioxide gas that made it rise. **FIG. 12.**

10. Divide the dough into twelve pieces of equal size by pinching off pieces of dough. Form each piece into a smooth ball and put the dough balls back in the bowl. **FIG. 13.**

11. Grease the sheet pan with butter or cover it with parchment paper.

12. Place the dough balls on the sheet pan, equally spaced. At this point, you can shape them into monsters or animals by clipping them with kitchen shears and adding dried fruit as eyes and noses. **FIG. 14.**

13. Cover the rolls with plastic wrap and let them rise again for about an hour or until they've doubled in size. When the rolls have almost finished rising, preheat oven to 375°F (190°C, or gas mark 5). To give them a shiny finish, beat an egg and brush it onto the rolls (optional).

14. Check the plastic zipper bag again to see how much gas was produced by the growing yeast. Open the bag to release the pressure and throw the bag and yeast away. **FIG. 15.**

15. Bake the rolls at 375°F (190°C, or gas mark 5) for 15 to 20 minutes, until they are light brown and the center is done. Eat your science experiment. **FIG. 16.**

THE SCIENCE BEHIND THE FUN

Yeasts are microbes called fungi. Thanks to yeast, humans have been making bread for more than 4,000 years. Yeast cells need energy to grow and multiply. They love to eat sugar and starches, like the ones in bread flour. As they eat and grow, yeast cells produce carbon dioxide gas. This is the same gas that makes the plastic bag in this lab puff up.

In bread dough, carbon dioxide gas from yeast makes tiny bubbles that make the bread rise. The bubbles pop during baking, leaving the small holes you see in bread. The active bread yeast usually used for baking is dried and can't grow until you add water to it.

FIG. 1 Materials

FIG. 2 Mix butter, sugar, and salt.

FIG. 3 Beat two eggs into the mixture.

FIG. 4 Stir in warm milk.

FIG. 5 Add flour and yeast.

FIG. 6 Mix until you have a shaggy ball of dough.

FIG. 7 Scrape the dough onto a sheet pan dusted with flour.

FIG. 8 Knead dough for 5 minutes or so.

FIG. 9 Cover the dough with plastic wrap or a damp towel and let it rise.

FIG. 10 While the dough rises, add water, yeast, and sugar to a zipper bag.

FIG. 11 Squeeze any air out of the bag and set it beside the rising dough.

FIG. 12 After 45 minutes, punch excess gas out of the dough and check the plastic bag of yeast.

FIG. 13 Form the dough into twelve small balls.

FIG. 14 Shape the dough balls into beasts and use kitchen shears to add details.

FIG. 15 Check the plastic bag again and let the carbon dioxide gas out so that it doesn't explode. Throw the bag away.

FIG. 16 Bake the yeast rolls at 375°F (190°C, or gas mark 5) and then eat your science experiment.

LAB 15
KALEIDOSCOPIC EGGS

Use food coloring and vinegar to create colorful patterns on hard-boiled eggs.

MATERIALS FIG. I

Raw egg

Sheet pan

Hard-boiled white eggs (Alternatively, brown, blue, or green eggs can be soaked in vinegar for 15 minutes and rubbed with a paper towel to expose the lighter shell underneath.)

Vinegar

Paper towels

Spoon

Food coloring of your choice

Rubber bands (optional)

Coarse salt, such as kosher salt

Dish gloves or disposable gloves (optional)

Bowl

Water

SAFETY TIPS AND HINTS

✱ Gloves will protect hands from food coloring.

✱ Neon food coloring works well for this project.

PROTOCOL

1. To test the strength of an eggshell, hold a raw egg over a sheet pan and squeeze it as hard as you can. Chances are you won't be able to break it with your bare hand. (Remove rings before squeezing the raw egg.)

2. Place several hard-boiled eggs in a bowl and cover them with vinegar for 15 minutes. Observe the carbon dioxide bubbles that form as the shells react with the vinegar. **FIG. 2.**

3. Cover a sheet pan with paper towels. **FIG. 3.**

4. Use a spoon to remove the eggs from the vinegar and place them on the paper towels. Drip food coloring onto the eggs. **FIG. 4.**

5. If you want lines on the eggs, stretch rubber bands around them before adding food coloring to prevent the dye from reaching the covered areas. **FIG. 5.**

6. Create multiple colors and patterns on the eggs. Use a spoon to turn the eggs, if you want to dye the underside.

7. Sprinkle coarse salt onto some of the dyed eggs to see what happens. **FIG. 6.**

8. When you have finished, let the food coloring sit on the eggs for around 30 minutes.

9. Put gloves on, if you have them. Fill a bowl with water and dip the eggs in the water to rinse off excess dye. Allow the eggs to dry on a paper towel. **FIG. 7.**

10. The color stays on the shells because food coloring is a chemical called an acid dye, and vinegar is an acid that helps the food coloring stick to the eggshells. **FIG. 8.**

11. Peel one of the kaleidoscopic eggs. Did the food coloring move all the way through the shell?

THE SCIENCE BEHIND THE FUN

Chicken eggs are delicate and incredibly strong at the same time. This is important for developing chicks because eggs must be strong enough for hens to sit on yet fragile enough to allow chicks to peck their way out. Thanks to their arched shape and crystalline structure, eggshells accomplish both goals.

Two chemical elements—calcium and carbon—bind together to form the calcium carbonate crystals in eggshells. When vinegar (acetic acid) is added to eggshells, a chemical reaction occurs. The crystals break up, and one of the products from the reaction is the carbon dioxide bubbles you observe in this lab.

Food coloring is what scientists call an **acid dye**. The dye molecules are attracted to the vinegar on the eggshells and form a bond with the shell. Salt is a hygroscopic (water-absorbing) chemical that pulls the moisture away from the eggshell, creating lighter spots on the colorful surface.

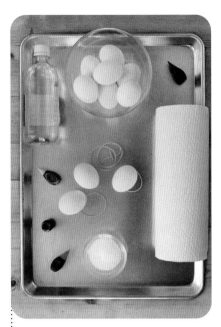

FIG. 1 Materials

FIG. 2 Cover hard-boiled eggs with vinegar.

FIG. 3 Add a layer of paper towels to a sheet pan.

FIG. 4 After 15 minutes, put the eggs on the paper towels and drip food coloring onto the shells.

FIG. 5 Before you add food coloring, you can put rubber bands on some of the eggs to create lines.

FIG. 6 Sprinkle salt on a few eggs to see what happens.

FIG. 7 When you are done adding color, briefly rinse the eggs in a bowl of water and put them back on the paper towels to dry.

FIG. 8 Vinegar is an acid that helps the food coloring stick to the eggshells.

MATERIAL SCIENCE

Sprinkles, Gelatin, and Non-Newtonian Goo

A material is defined as the matter from which things can be made. Materials are used for countless applications—from building houses, cars, and computers to making the perfect dessert. The sheet pans used in this book are made from metal. The term "material" is most often used to describe solids but can be used to describe other useful objects as well.

Material scientists study the different properties of materials. They are interested in how these properties are determined by a material's structure and makeup. For example, it is useful to understand how well a material conducts electricity or heat, how flexible it is, or how it vibrates when exposed to sound waves.

In this unit, you will play with some useful materials, including salt, gelatin, crystals, cornstarch, and sugar sprinkles. As you experiment, think about applications for the materials you are studying. What could a non-Newtonian fluid—a rule-breaking substance—such as cornstarch goo be used for? Why is it important to understand how sound waves affect different materials, and why is it helpful to know how salt affects ice?

LAB 16

CORNSTARCH GOO

MESS FACTOR	COMPLEXITY
high	*low*

Stir up a batch of strange non-Newtonian fluid that acts like both a liquid and a solid.

MATERIALS FIG.1

Bowl
Sheet pan
Spoon (optional)

1 cup (128 g) cornstarch
½ cup (120 ml) water
Watercolor paints (optional)

Paintbrush (optional)

SAFETY TIPS AND HINTS

✶ To fill an entire half-sheet with goo, double or triple the recipe.

✶ This project cleans up easily with water.

PROTOCOL

1. Set a bowl on a sheet pan.

2. In the bowl, use a spoon or your hands to mix the cornstarch and water. Add water and cornstarch as needed until the goo is the consistency of thick syrup. **FIG. 2.**

3. Pour the cornstarch goo onto a sheet pan. **FIG. 3.**

4. Roll some of the cornstarch mixture into a ball. **FIG. 4.**

5. Stop moving it around and let it drip between your fingers. **FIG. 5.**

6. See what happens when you slap your hand down on it. **FIG. 6**, **FIG. 7.**

7. Paint on the goo to see whether the paint stays in place or spreads out over time. **FIG. 8.**

THE SCIENCE BEHIND THE FUN

Most fluids and solids behave in expected ways. Solids remain solid when you push, pull, squeeze, and shake them. Fluids flow and take the shape of the containers that hold them. However, some fluids, known as non-Newtonian fluids, don't follow the rules.

Cornstarch and water mix together to form what scientists call a **shear-thickening fluid**. When you apply stress to it by moving it around or slapping it, the atoms in the cornstarch rearrange to make it act more like a solid. That's why, when you let the goo sit in the palm of your hand or let it slowly slide between your fingers, it acts like liquid, but if you squeeze it, stir it, or roll it around in your hands, it behaves more like a solid.

FIG. 1 Materials

FIG. 2 Add water to the cornstarch.

FIG. 3 Mix the cornstarch solution well and pour it onto a sheet pan.

FIG. 4 Roll the goo into a ball or let it drip between your fingers.

FIG. 5 Observe the long strands that form as the fluid flows.

FIG. 6 Slap the goo to see whether it will splash.

FIG. 7 If the cornstarch mixture gets too dry, add a little more water.

FIG. 8 Use watercolor paint to turn the goo into a piece of art.

LAB 17
CRYSTAL GARDEN

MESS FACTOR
medium

COMPLEXITY
low

Use a supersaturated Epsom salt solution to grow a garden of sparkling crystals.

MATERIALS FIG. 1

Several small wide-mouthed jars or recycled plastic bottles
Scissors (optional)
Sheet pan
3 cups (864 g) Epsom salt
2 cups (473 ml) water

Large microwavable container or pot
Microwave or stovetop
Pipe cleaners (chenille stems) and small pom-poms (optional)
Wooden skewers, cut in half
Green food coloring
Magnifying glass or camera (optional)

SAFETY TIPS AND HINTS

✢ An adult should supervise dissolving salt in hot water.

✢ Allow the Epsom salt solution to cool to a safe temperature before pouring.

✢ A half-sheet pan works well for this lab.

PROTOCOL

1. If using recycled plastic bottles, use scissors to cut the tops off so that they are around 2 inches (5 to 6 cm) tall. **FIG. 2.**

2. Set jars or bottles on a sheet pan.

3. Add Epsom salt to the water and heat in the microwave or on a stove until the solution is clear and all the salts are dissolved. **FIG. 3.**

4. Allow the salts to cool to a safe temperature.

5. While the salts cool, make pipe cleaner flowers with stems around 6 inches (15 cm) long. Pom-poms can be incorporated at the center of the petals. The flowers should be small enough to fit easily into the bottles or jars. **FIG. 4.**

6. Bend the flower stems around wooden skewers so the tops of the flowers are suspended about 0.4 inches (1 cm) above the bottom of the containers.

7. When the solution has cooled, add it to the bottles so that it just covers the flowers but not the stems. Pour any leftover solution into the bottom of the pan. **FIG. 5.**

8. Drip green food coloring into the Epsom salt solution in the bottom of the pan to create "grass" around the garden. **FIG. 6.**

9. Let the garden sit for several hours, checking on the crystal growth every half hour or so.

10. When long, needlelike crystals have grown on the flowers, carefully remove them from the containers. Twist the stems around the skewers and flip them over so that they are sitting in the containers with the blossoms up. **FIG. 7**, **FIG. 8.**

11. Study the crystals under a magnifying glass or photograph the crystal flowers and enlarge the photos for a close-up view.

THE SCIENCE BEHIND THE FUN

Epsom salt contains the chemical magnesium sulfate. Adding this salt to very hot water makes it possible for the water to hold far more dissolved salt than it normally would at room temperature. Scientists call solutions like the one you make in this lab supersaturated solutions.

As the salt solution cools, some of the magnesium sulfate molecules stick to the pipe cleaner bristles. Other magnesium sulfate molecules snap onto those molecules like puzzle pieces, creating a repeating, three-dimensional pattern called a **crystal**. As more and more salt molecules snap on, the crystals become larger and larger. Although their sizes may vary, they all have the same shape.

The salt in the pan creates needlelike crystals as well, but they form along the bottom of the pan to create a beautiful flat mosaic.

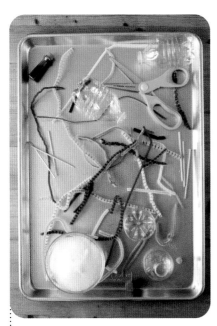

FIG. I Materials

FIG. 2 Cut the tops off some plastic water bottles to create small, clear cups.

FIG. 3 Dissolve Epsom salts in the water.

FIG. 4 Use pipe cleaners to make small flowers and suspend them in the cups using skewers or pencils.

FIG. 5 Pour Epsom salt solution into the cups to cover the flowers. Add leftover liquid to the bottom of the sheet pan.

FIG. 6 Add several drops of green food coloring to the salt solution in the pan to create crystal "grass" for the garden.

FIG. 7 When the crystals have grown, remove the flowers from the cups.

FIG. 8 Wind the stems around the skewers to make a crystal bouquet.

LAB 18
ICE FISHING

Use a string and some salt to catch frozen cubes.

MESS FACTOR
low

COMPLEXITY
low

MATERIALS FIG. 1

Stick or skewer
Piece of cotton kitchen twine or yarn, about 6 inches
   (15 cm) long
Water

Sheet pan
Ice cubes
Salt

SAFETY TIPS AND HINTS

It may take practice to perfect your ice fishing technique, so if it doesn't work the first time, try again.

PROTOCOL

1. Cut the sharp end off of a stick or skewer. Tie kitchen twine around one end of the stick or skewer to create a small "fishing pole." **FIG. 2.**

2. Add a few inches of water to the bottom of a sheet pan to create a pond. **FIG. 3.**

3. Add several ice cubes to the pan so that they're sitting in the water. **FIG. 4.**

4. Soak the string on your fishing pole in water. **FIG. 5.**

5. Try to pick an ice cube up by placing the string on top of it and pulling.

6. Lay the string across several ice cubes and sprinkle a generous amount of salt over the string and ice cubes. **FIG. 6.**

7. Wait a minute or two and try to lift the cube using only the string. Did you catch some ice? **FIG. 7, FIG. 8.**

THE SCIENCE BEHIND THE FUN

Table salt is a chemical called **sodium chloride**. Humans have been using it for thousands of years, and before refrigerators and freezers were around, salting meat was one of the only ways to preserve it. Today, salt is still a delicious and important food seasoning, but it is also used to melt ice on roads in the wintertime.

Normally, ice melts and water freezes at 32°F (0°C). Luckily, salt lowers the temperature at which ice melts and water freezes. That means that sodium chloride and other salts can be added to roads to melt ice when it is below freezing outside.

In this experiment, you add salt to the ice cube that a string is sitting on. The salt causes the ice surrounding the string to melt, stealing heat from the surrounding water. The cold water created by melting salt then refreezes around the string. Soon the string is trapped in ice, and the ice cubes can be lifted from the water.

Different chemicals change the freezing point of water at different temperatures. While table salt can thaw ice at 15°F (-9°C), it doesn't work at 0°F (-18°C). Other deicing chemicals melt ice at much colder temperatures, down to -10°F (-23°C) degrees below zero.

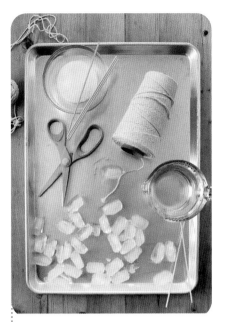

FIG. 1 Materials

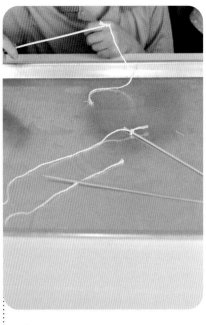

FIG. 2 Tie cotton twine to sticks to make ice fishing rods.

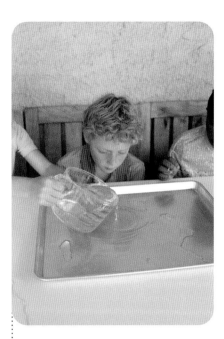

FIG. 3 Fill a sheet pan with water.

FIG. 4 Add ice cubes to the water.

FIG. 5 Wet the cotton twine in the water and then lay it across some ice cubes.

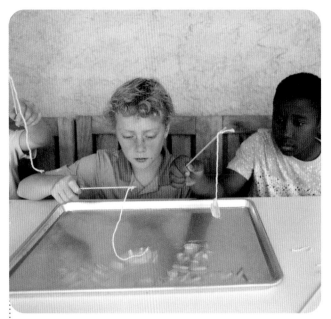

FIG. 6 Sprinkle a generous pinch of salt on the string where it is touching the ice cubes.

FIG. 7 Wait a minute or two and lift the string out of the water.

FIG. 8 The salt causes the ice to melt and water to refreeze around the string.

LAB 19
SHRINKING WINDOW GELS

MESS FACTOR
medium

COMPLEXITY
medium

Make colorful window decorations that shrink as they dry and see what happens when food coloring molecules diffuse (move) through gelatin.

MATERIALS FIG.1

4 cups (1 L) water
Microwave or stovetop
Microwaveable container or pot for boiling water
6 packs (1 ounce, or 4 grams each) plain, unflavored gelatin

Spoon
Sheet pan
Table knife
Parchment paper or waxed paper
Wide spatula
Small, simple cookie cutters

Toothpicks
Food coloring of your choice
Ruler (optional)

SAFETY TIPS AND HINTS

✹ An adult should supervise dissolving the gelatin in hot water.

✹ One recipe will fill a full-sheet pan or two half-sheets.

✹ Kids may need help transferring gelatin to parchment paper.

✹ Simple cookie cutter shapes work best since gelatin is fragile.

PROTOCOL

1. Boil the water in the microwave or on the stove. Add the gelatin to the boiling water. Stir well until all the gelatin has dissolved. You may need to keep microwaving at short intervals. Remove large bubbles with a spoon. **FIG. 2.**

2. Let the gelatin cool to a kid-safe temperature. Pour the liquid gelatin onto a sheet pan so that it is approximately 0.4 inches (1 cm) deep.

3. Allow the gelatin to solidify.

4. Use a table knife to cut the gelatin into squares large enough for a cookie cutter to fit inside. **FIG. 3.**

5. Pour a small amount of water over the knife marks and allow the water to loosen the gelatin from the pan. **FIG. 4.**

6. Line a second sheet pan or a plate with parchment paper or waxed paper.

7. Carefully, use a wide spatula or your fingers to transfer the gelatin squares to the parchment paper.

8. Use cookie cutters to cut shapes from the squares and remove the surrounding gelatin. **FIG. 5.**

9. Dip toothpicks in food coloring to create colorful designs by poking food coloring into the gelatin. Try not to poke all the way through. **FIG. 6.**

10. Gently remove the gelatin shapes from the parchment paper and stick them to a window. **FIG. 7.**

11. Check the window gels every few hours to observe the food coloring as it diffuses (spreads out) in the gelatin. Record your observations. Do some colors diffuse faster than others?

12. Observe the gels each day to see what happens when the water evaporates from the gelatin. When the gels are dry, peel them off the window. **FIG. 8.**

13. If you'd like to make them soft again, rehydrate the gelatin by soaking the dried shapes in water.

THE SCIENCE BEHIND THE FUN

When gelatin is heated and dissolved in water, it acts like a liquid, but it cools down to form a jiggly, sticky gel. This suspension of tiny particles in water is called a **hydrocolloid**. Over time, as water evaporates from the gelatin, it shrinks and becomes a solid.

If you poke liquid food coloring into solidified gelatin, the dye will start to move from areas where there is lots of food coloring to areas where there is less food coloring. Scientists call this type of movement **diffusion**, and many things can affect how quickly chemicals move from one place to another. Diffusion takes place in gases like air, liquids like water, and even solids.

When molecules are heated up, they move around faster, and cool temperatures slow them down. If you put this experiment in the refrigerator, the dots would expand more slowly. Small molecules can move through gelatin more quickly than large ones. That's why some colors that contain smaller chemical dyes might move more quickly through gelatin than colors made up of larger chemical units.

FIG. 1 Materials

FIG. 2 Dissolve gelatin in boiling water and pour onto a sheet pan.

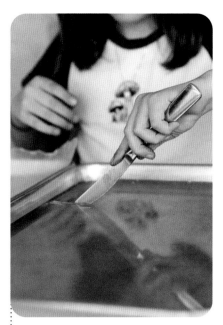

FIG. 3 When the gelatin is solid, cut it into large squares.

FIG. 4 Pour some water along the cut marks to help loosen the gelatin from the pan.

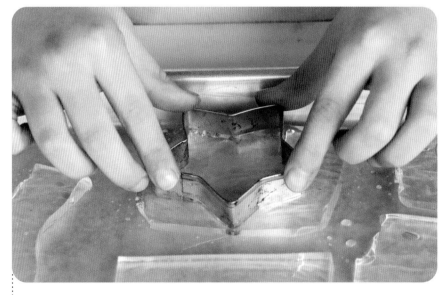

FIG. 5 With a spatula, carefully move the gelatin squares to a piece of parchment paper. Cut shapes from the gelatin.

FIG. 6 Poke toothpicks dipped in food coloring into the gelatin shapes to decorate them.

FIG. 7 Gently stick the gelatin shapes to a window and observe what happens to the food coloring over time.

FIG. 8 When the window gels are dry, remove them from the window.

LAB 20
DANCING SPRINKLES

MESS FACTOR
medium

COMPLEXITY
low

Use sound waves to make baking sprinkles jump around.

MATERIALS FIG. 1

Online tone generator website or app with a slide bar for changing tone

Device such as a cell phone that can be linked to speaker

Wireless speaker

Plastic bin or bowl large enough to hold the speaker

Sheet pan

Plastic wrap

Tape or a large rubber band

Baking sprinkles or sesame seeds

Water

Eyedropper (optional)

SAFETY TIPS AND HINTS

Remember to turn the speaker on and pair it to an external device before covering it with plastic wrap.

PROTOCOL

1. Upload a tone generator website or app to a phone or another device. A tone generator with a slide bar works best so you can change the tone smoothly and easily.

2. Turn a small wireless speaker on and pair it to the device. **FIG. 2.**

3. Place a plastic bin or large bowl on a sheet pan and place the speaker in the bin.

4. Cover the bin or bowl with plastic wrap. Use tape or a large rubber band to secure the plastic wrap. Make it tight and smooth, like the top of a drum. **FIG. 3.**

5. Put baking sprinkles or sesame seeds on the plastic wrap. **FIG. 4.**

6. Turn the tone generator on at a medium volume. Start with the lowest tone (frequency or pitch, which is measured in hertz) and slowly slide the bar to the right to increase the pitch. Observe what happens to the sprinkles. **FIG. 5.**

7. Note the frequency (in hertz) at which the sprinkles jumped the highest. **FIG. 6.**

8. Play some music with loud bass parts through the speaker to make the sprinkles dance to the music.

9. Remove the sprinkles from the plastic and drip some water onto the pan. **FIG. 7.**

10. Use the tone generator to see how sound waves affect the water sitting on the plastic. **FIG. 8.**

11. Note the frequency (in hertz) where waves form and the frequency where water jumped from the surface.

12. Compare the frequencies that made the sprinkles and the water jump around. Were they the same? Test sprinkles of different sizes to compare their response to varying pitches.

THE SCIENCE BEHIND THE FUN

When objects vibrate in the air, air molecules are squashed together to create repeating pressure waves. We call these pressure waves **sound**. Electrical speakers translate electrical energy into sound by moving mechanical parts back and forth to create pressure waves (sound).

Frequency, or pitch, is the number of times per second that a sound pressure wave repeats itself. An electric bass has a much lower frequency than a piccolo. Frequency is measured in hertz (Hz), the number of pressure waves per second that move past a fixed point.

Every object has a natural **frequency** at which it "wants" to vibrate. In this lab, at certain pitches, the vibrations are at the right frequencies to make sprinkles jump and wave patterns to form in water.

In your ear, sound energy is translated into electrical signals. Humans have a thin membrane in our ears called an **eardrum**, similar to the tight plastic wrap in this lab. The eardrum detects sound waves from the air and vibrates, sending vibrations to the middle ear and then on to the inner ear where they are translated into electrical signals that travel to our brain.

FIG. 1 Materials

FIG. 2 Pair a wireless speaker to a device, such as a phone.

FIG. 3 Place the speaker in a bin on a sheet pan and cover the bin with plastic wrap. Secure the plastic with tape.

FIG. 4 Put some sprinkles on the plastic wrap.

FIG. 5 Play a tone generator through the speaker, changing the volume and tone to see how the sprinkles react.

FIG. 6 Do they jump higher from the vibrations of a low pitch or a high pitch?

FIG. 7 Remove the sprinkles and add a few drops of water to the plastic wrap.

FIG. 8 Repeat the experiment to see what happens. Look for wave patterns in the water.

NATURAL SCIENCE

Sprouts, Dyes, and Eco Prints

There are two main branches of natural science. Life science is the scientific study of living organisms, including microorganisms, plants, and animals. The other branch is physical science, which is concerned with matter that isn't alive, such as rocks and chemicals.

The two branches are tightly interwoven. Living things are dependent on nonliving matter to create an environment containing the things required for life. Without nonliving matter such as nutrients, air, water, and rock, life as we know it would not exist.

In this unit, you will experiment with seeds, plants, and materials made from plants, such as dye and paper. It's fun to use some of the colorful pigments produced by plants to dye fabric. Creating sun prints illustrates how the life-giving sun can cause chemical changes in organic matter such as paper. Growing sprouts from seeds is a live demonstration of the process of germination, offering us a glimpse into just one of the many wonderful processes of life on Earth.

LAB 21
FABULOUS FABRIC DYE

MESS FACTOR	COMPLEXITY

medium	*high*

Dye fabric in vivid hues using alum, black beans, and onion skins.

MATERIALS FIG.1

Large bowls

16 oz (454 g) bag dried black beans

Water

Several yellow onions

Large, old cooking pot reserved for craft projects (see "Safety Tips and Hints")

Kitchen scale (optional)

Laundry detergent (washing soda, if possible)

1.9 oz (53 g) alum (aluminum sulfate), available online and in the spice section of grocery stores

Chopstick or old spoon for mixing alum

100 percent cotton dish towels, T-shirts, or other items (wool or silk will also work)

Rubber dish gloves or medical gloves

Lemon (optional)

Sheet pan

Rubber bands or kitchen twine

Cardboard (optional)

Plastic wrap (optional)

"Iron water" (optional; see Lab 25)

Leaves

Large stick or thick dowel for eco prints (optional)

SAFETY TIPS AND HINTS

★ This project can be performed without using alum by simply dyeing untreated fabric with the dyes you make. However, results may vary.

★ Alum will contaminate cooking vessels with aluminum, so don't use a pot that you cook with for the fabric pretreatment step.

★ Yellow onion dye will retain its color when you wash it. Black bean dye will fade to blue-gray, and pink lemon spots will turn white when washed.

PROTOCOL

PREPARE BLACK BEAN DYE

1. In a large bowl, cover black beans with water and soak for 6 to 12 hours. Keep adding water so that beans remain covered. **FIG. 2.**

2. Strain out beans and reserve the blue water that remains. Save the beans for cooking.

PREPARE YELLOW ONION DYE

1. Peel the yellow-orange skin from the outside of several onions.

2. Add onion peels to a cooking pot, cover them with water, and simmer for an hour or so.

3. Strain out onion skins.

PREPARE FABRIC

1. If you have a kitchen scale, weigh the items you wish to dye and record the weight.

2. Wash items you want to dye in laundry detergent or washing soda to remove any chemicals on the fibers.

3. Fill a large, old cooking pot halfway to two-thirds full of water. If you did not weigh the fabric, add all of the alum to the water and bring to a simmer. If you weighed the fabric, calculate 10 percent of the weight and add that much alum. (For example, if the fabric weighs 15 oz [425 g], add 1.5 oz [42.5 g] alum to the water.)

4. Stir alum solution and add fabric. Simmer for an hour. Let cool.

5. Wearing gloves, remove fabric from alum and squeeze out excess water. Hang up to dry or dye immediately.

6. **To dye fabric a solid color:** Soak alum-treated cotton in dye for at least 1 hour. Dry. To make lemon prints, cut a lemon in half and use it to stamp on the black bean–dyed cloth. Citric acid in the lemon will react with the pigment in the dye to turn the cloth pink. **FIG. 3.**

7. **To create a spiral tie-dye pattern:** Lay the cloth on a sheet pan. Grab it in the middle and start twisting. Continue twisting until you have a fabric spiral. Use four rubber bands or pieces of twine to separate the spiral into eight pie-shaped pieces. On the pan, soak every other segment or every two segments with dye, alternating blue and yellow, blue and white, or yellow and white. **FIG. 4, FIG. 5.**

8. **To create a triangle tie-dye pattern:** Fold fabric in half the long way and then fold it in half again until you have a narrow piece of cloth. Fold one corner of the cloth over to make a triangle and continue folding until you are left with a folded triangle. Cut two pieces of cardboard into triangles to fit the fabric. Put a cardboard triangle on each side and use rubber bands or twine to attach the cardboard to the cloth. On the sheet pan, soak the exposed sides of the cloth with fabric dye. **FIG. 6, FIG. 7.**

9. If tie-dyeing, wrap the dyed cloth in plastic wrap. Place it on the sheet pan and set it out in the sun for several hours. Alternatively, let it sit at room temperature overnight. When the time is up, remove plastic wrap and rubber bands. Unfold the cloth to reveal designs. Dry the fabric. **FIG. 8.**

10. Fabric may be framed, rinsed, or washed. Do not put black bean– and onion–dyed fabric with other laundry the first time you wash it. Remember: The yellow dye will stay yellow, but the blue of the black bean dye will turn blue-gray when it reacts with laundry detergent.

BONUS ACTIVITY: MAKE ECO PRINTS ON ALUM-TREATED, COTTON, OR DYED FABRIC

1. Make rusty "iron water" (see Lab 25). Add several tablespoons of rusty water to a gallon of clean water in an old container.

2. Lay fabric flat on a sheet pan.

3. Position leaves on fabric. **FIG. 9.**

4. Soak a second piece of fabric in the gallon of iron water. **FIG. 10.**

5. Lay the soaked fabric flat over the leaves. **FIG. 11.**

6. Roll the two layers of fabric tightly around a stick or dowel. Wind kitchen twine tightly around the fabric roll. **FIG. 12, FIG. 13.**

7. For color, add dye to the cloth (optional). Wrap in plastic wrap and leave in direct sunlight on a hot day. For darker leaf prints, steam the fabric roll as in Lab 25 on a baking rack and sheet pan covered in foil, with a little bit of water. **FIG. 14.**

8. Unwrap the fabric to reveal leaf prints. Read more about the science in Lab 25. **FIG. 15, FIG. 16.**

THE SCIENCE BEHIND THE FUN

Plant dyes are organic (carbon-containing) chemicals that absorb certain light waves and reflect others. If a piece of fabric is dyed yellow, it will reflect yellow light waves and absorb all other visible colors, including red, green, and blue. Because human eyes can only detect reflected light, we see a yellow piece of fabric.

A mordant such as alum (aluminum sulfate) is a substance that combines with dyes and fixes them to a material. Soaking cotton in the alum solution allows a weak bond to form between the fabric and the alum.

Certain dyes, such as black bean dye, contain chemicals that change color when you put them in detergent or in acids, such as lemon juice.

FIG. I Materials

FIG. 2 Soak black beans and boil onion skins to make dye.

FIG. 3 For solid colors, soak alum-treated cotton in dye for several hours.

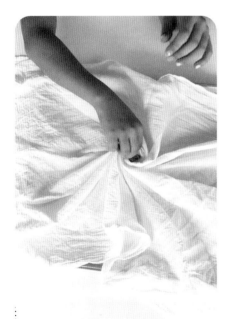

FIG. 4 For tie-dye, twist fabric into a tight spiral.

FIG. 5 Secure the spiral with rubber bands and soak alternating sections with dye.

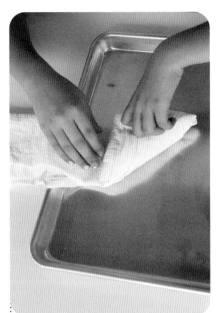

FIG. 6 Create a triangular pattern by accordion-folding fabric and then folding triangles.

FIG. 7 Cover fabric triangle with cardboard on both sides. Secure with rubber bands and soak each side with dye.

FIG. 8 After several hours, remove the rubber bands to reveal the design you created.

FIG. 9 To make leaf prints, add leaves to fabric on a sheet pan.

FIG. 10 Soak a second piece of fabric in iron water (see Lab 25). Wring out excess water.

FIG. 11 Lay the iron water-treated fabric over the leaves.

FIG. 12 Tightly roll the fabric and leaves on a stick or dowel.

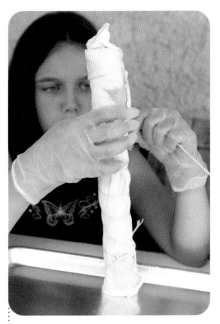

FIG. 13 Wrap kitchen twine or yarn around the roll as tightly as possible.

FIG. 14 For color, add dye to the cloth. Cover with plastic wrap and leave in direct sunlight for several hours. For darker prints, do not wrap; instead, steam the roll of fabric on a sheet pan (see Lab 25).

FIG. 15 When fabric is ready, unwrap and remove the leaves to see the leaf prints.

FIG. 16 Hang fabric up to dry.

LAB 22
SPROUT GARDEN

MESS FACTOR	COMPLEXITY
medium	*low*

Watch germination in action by growing living art on a sheet pan.

MATERIALS FIG.1

Sheet pan
Potting soil
Trowel or large spoon

Kitchen twine or yarn
Seeds (a variety, if possible)
Camera

Paper and pencil
Spray bottle or watering can
Magnifying glass

SAFETY TIPS AND HINTS

If using edible sprouts for this project, wash them well before consuming. Sprouts can be breeding grounds for bacteria that cause food poisoning.

PROTOCOL

1. Cover the bottom of the sheet pan with potting soil so that it is around 0.4 inches (1 cm) deep. **FIG. 2.**

2. Use kitchen twine to make designs on the soil. **FIG. 3.**

3. Put seeds in small containers labeled with the type of seeds they hold. **FIG. 4.**

4. Sprinkle the seeds densely into the design, keeping different types of seed separated with the string. **FIG. 5.**

5. Take a photo of the seed design and use paper and a pencil to make a map of what seeds you planted in each area. **FIG. 6.**

6. Cover the seeds with a layer of soil. **FIG. 7.**

7. Use a spray bottle or watering can to soak the soil until it is uniformly damp.

8. Water the seeds daily or when the soil looks dry.

9. Observe the seeds as they sprout. Use your map to record the date and time each type of sprout emerges. **FIG. 8.**

10. Use a camera or magnifying glass to observe the sprouts close up. Note differences in shape, height, and color of the sprouts. Record your observations.

THE SCIENCE BEHIND THE FUN

Seeds contain baby plants that are dormant (not growing). These embryonic plants need certain signals to make them "wake up" and emerge. The changes a seed goes through as it sprouts and forms leaves is called germination. Light, air, and water are all environmental signals that allow germination to begin. Temperature can also be important.

How quickly the seeds in this lab germinate depends on how well they like the environmental conditions provided by the light, moisture, and temperature in the soil and the room where they are growing. Some seeds take longer to germinate because they have thick, tough seed coats that protect them under dry conditions. Seeds like this can be presoaked in water to make them germinate more quickly.

When a plant first sprouts, it gets all the nutrients it needs from the seed, and the seed shrinks as the plant grows. As it matures, a plant depends on roots and leaves to collect the water, nutrients, and sunlight it requires.

FIG. 1 Materials

FIG. 2 Fill a sheet pan with soil.

FIG. 3 Use kitchen twine or yarn to make designs on the dirt.

FIG. 4 Put seeds in small containers labeled with the types of seeds.

FIG. 5 Sprinkle the seeds densely on the soil.

FIG. 6 Take a photo of the seeds and make a map of the garden.

FIG. 7 Cover the seeds with a thin layer of soil and water.

FIG. 8 Observe how long it takes each type of seed to sprout and grow.

LAB 23
LIVING PAPER

MESS FACTOR	COMPLEXITY
medium	*low*

Learn how paper is made by converting everyday paper into seed-studded paper that will sprout in soil.

MATERIALS FIG. 1

Inexpensive heavy white paper, such as craft paper or watercolor paper
Scissors or paper shredder
Bowl
Water
Blender
Colander with flat bottom
Sheet pan

Spoon
Wildflower or herb seeds (collected from outside or from a seed pack)
Jar lids from canning jars
Herbs (optional)
Flower petals (optional)
Parchment paper (optional)

SAFETY TIPS AND HINTS

✶ Adult supervision is recommended when using a blender and paper shredder.

✶ Dry living paper immediately. To prevent molding and sprouting, do not seal the paper in plastic bags.

PROTOCOL

1. Shred paper using scissors or a paper shredder.

2. In a bowl, soak the paper in water for an hour or more.

3. Transfer the wet paper to a blender and add some water. Blend the paper to a fine pulp. **FIG. 2.**

4. Set a colander over a bowl on a sheet pan. Use a spoon to add the paper pulp to the colander and squeeze out the excess water. Discard the water and put the pulp in the bowl or divide into two bowls.

5. Stir wildflower or herb seeds into the pulp. Save a few for decoration. **FIG. 3.**

6. Place a jar lid in the colander.

7. Press the paper pulp into the lid to create a paper disk. Squeeze out any excess water. Put the lid on the sheet pan. **FIG. 4.**

8. Add extra seeds and herbs or petals for decoration and for indicating what type of seed is contained in the disk. **FIG. 5.**

9. Press any leftover paper pulp onto parchment paper on a sheet pan and decorate with petals or leaves. **FIG. 6, FIG. 7.**

10. Let the seed paper dry for several days. Remove disks from the jar lids.

11. Punch holes in the paper if you'd like to use them as gift tags.

12. Plant the disks by covering them with soil and watering as needed. **FIG. 8.**

THE SCIENCE BEHIND THE FUN

Today, most paper is made from plant fibers that have been ground up and formed into flat sheets. In this lab, you recycle paper by adding water and using a blender to chew it into a pulp. It's fun to see how paper fibers absorb water, allowing you to reshape them, and how the pulp changes as water evaporates and the fibers dry out.

Seeds are alive. They are immature plants covered by a protective coat that keeps them safe until they detect the moisture, warmth, and sunlight needed to sprout. Because seeds contain all the nutrients needed for sending out roots, a shoot, and leaves, seeds shrink as baby plants consume the energy within.

The living paper in this experiment helps protect the seeds and keeps them dry until you plant them. Once the seeds sprout, paper forms a nice foundation for young plants because it holds in moisture and allows roots to take hold.

FIG. 1 Materials

FIG. 2 Blend wet, shredded paper. Press out extra water.

FIG. 3 Add seeds to paper pulp and mix.

FIG. 4 Press paper pulp into jar lids, squeezing out extra water.

FIG. 5 Decorate the paper with petals or herbs, depending on the seeds.

FIG. 6 Paper pulp can be pressed flat onto parchment paper and decorated with petals and leaves on both sides.

FIG. 7 Decorative paper without seeds can be speed-dried in the oven at 170°F (77°C). Do not bake paper containing seeds.

FIG. 8 Put the living paper in soil and cover with more dirt and water to make the seeds sprout and grow.

LAB 24
SUN PRINTS

Create sun prints by using the ultraviolet rays in sunlight to break down chemicals in construction paper.

MATERIALS FIG. 1

Brightly colored construction paper (inexpensive construction paper works best)

Sheet pan
Leaves or stencil
Plastic wrap

Tape (optional)
Rocks (optional)

SAFETY TIPS AND HINTS

This lab gives the best results on a clear day when the sun is almost directly overhead.

PROTOCOL

1. Place two pieces of construction paper on a sheet pan. Blue, green, red, and black paper usually work well.

2. Arrange leaves or a stencil on the construction paper. **FIG. 2**, **FIG. 3.**

3. Cover the leaves and paper with plastic wrap. Tape it to the pan or weigh it down with rocks. **FIG. 4.**

4. Set the sheet pan in a sunny spot and leave it there for several hours. **FIG. 5**, **FIG. 6.**

5. After several hours in direct sunlight, remove the plastic and leaves or stencil to reveal the sun print. **FIG. 7.**

6. The ultraviolet rays in sunlight fade organic dyes in the paper, leaving a darker image where the paper was protected. **FIG. 8.**

7. Compare how ultraviolet fades paper on a cloudy day versus on a sunny day.

THE SCIENCE BEHIND THE FUN

The sun emits an enormous amount of energy, and some of it travels to Earth as light waves. Like waves moving across a lake, light waves can be different distances apart. Red light waves are spaced much farther apart than violet ones. Ultraviolet (UV) light waves are so close together that they cannot be detected by human eyes.

Most paper is made from plant fibers. When colorful paper is partially covered and put in sunlight, UV light destroys chemicals in the exposed paper, making the color appear lighter. The covered parts of the paper are protected from UV light and don't change color. Like paper, molecules in human skin can be damaged by UV light, which is why we wear sunscreen to block harmful UV rays.

FIG. 1 Materials

FIG. 2 Collect leaves, find a stencil, or cut shapes from paper.

FIG. 3 Place construction paper on a sheet pan and arrange the leaves or stencil on the paper.

FIG. 4 Cover the paper and leaves or stencil with plastic wrap. Tape or weigh down the plastic wrap.

FIG. 5 Set the sheet pan containing the paper in a sunny spot.

FIG. 6 Let the paper sit in the sun for several hours.

FIG. 7 Remove the plastic. Lift the leaves or stencil away from the paper to reveal the sun print.

FIG. 8 The darker areas on the sun prints indicate where the paper was protected from the sun's ultraviolet rays.

LAB 25
ECO ART

Create frame-worthy leaf prints from rusty water and foliage.

MATERIALS FIG.1

Steel wool
Vinegar
Jar
Water
Fresh leaves
Oven
Plastic bins
Wire cooling rack
Sheet pan
Scissors
Heavy paper, such as watercolor paper
Gloves or tongs
Paper towel
Heavy, flat-bottom dish, such as a casserole dish
Aluminum foil

MESS FACTOR
medium

COMPLEXITY
medium

SAFETY TIPS AND HINTS

✶ Large quantities of iron are poisonous if consumed, so do not drink the rusty water.

✶ An adult should remove the sheet pan from the oven after steaming the paper.

PROTOCOL

IRON WATER

1. Dip a piece of steel wool into vinegar. Remove the steel wool from the vinegar, place it in a jar, and allow it to rust overnight. Note how the temperature goes up inside the jar where the chemical reaction (oxidation) is occurring.

2. When the steel has rusted, add 1 tablespoon (15 ml) vinegar to the jar and fill it halfway with water.

3. This concentrated rusty water may be used right away, or you can allow it to sit for a few more days to get more rust in the water.

BOTANICAL PRINTS

1. Collect leaves such as maple, oak, and sumac , or whatever you can find.

2. Preheat oven to 350°F (180°C, or gas mark 4).

3. In a large container, add ½ cup (120 ml) vinegar to 4 cups (1.5 L) water.

4. Pour half the vinegar water into a second container and add 3 teaspoons (15 ml) of the rusty water to make "iron water."

5. Put a variety of leaves into the iron water to soak. **FIG. 2.**

6. Place a cooling rack on a sheet pan.

7. Cut heavy paper into pieces that will stack easily on the cooling rack.

8. Remove the leaves from the iron water and save them. Soak several sheets of heavy paper in the iron water mixture and several other sheets of paper in the water/vinegar mixture from step 3. **FIG. 3.**

9. Wearing disposable gloves or using tongs, remove a piece of paper from the water/vinegar solution. Place it on the cooling rack and blot it with a paper towel.

10. Arrange some of the iron water–soaked leaves on the water/vinegar paper, shiny-side down. **FIG. 4.**

11. Take a second piece of paper from the iron water/vinegar solution and place it on top of the leaves. **FIG. 5.**

12. Repeat if you wish and form a stack of paper and leaves, alternating sheets of water/vinegar and iron water/vinegar paper with leaves sandwiched in between.

13. Place a heavy flat object on the stack of paper. **FIG. 6.**

14. Cover the bottom of the sheet pan with an inch or so (about 3 cm) of water.

15. Use aluminum foil to cover everything tightly. Put the sheet pan in the oven.

16. Bake for 30 minutes to steam the paper and leaves. After 30 minutes, turn the oven off and let the pan and paper sit in the oven with the door closed for another 30 to 60 minutes. **FIG. 7.**

17. Carefully remove the pan from the oven, take the foil off, and reveal the eco prints. **FIG. 8.**

18. Allow the prints to dry and flatten them by pressing with a heavy object, if needed.

THE SCIENCE BEHIND THE FUN

Rusting is a type of chemical reaction called an oxidation reaction, which also occurs when something burns. Steel wool is mostly made up of iron along with a little bit of carbon. When the hydrogen and oxygen in water react with iron, red and brown chemical compounds containing iron and oxygen, called iron oxides, are formed. Vinegar speeds up the reaction.

While one side of a leaf is coated with a waxy substance, the underside contains tiny holes called stoma that allow water and gases to enter and exit. Leaves contain a green chemical called chlorophyll, which helps them convert water, sunlight, and carbon dioxide into energy. They also contain chemicals called tannins, which bind well to paper, iron, and fabric.

In this lab, tannins in the leaves react with iron compounds in rusty water. Adding heat to rusty water and leaves pressed against paper or fabric allows compounds formed by the iron and tannins to bind to the paper, creating beautiful images.

FIG. 1 Materials

FIG. 2 Add a few spoonfuls of rusty water to a mixture of water and vinegar to create "iron water." Add a variety of leaves to the iron water.

FIG. 3 Remove the leaves from the iron water and save them. Soak some sheets of heavy paper in the iron water mixture and some other sheets of paper in a water/vinegar mixture.

FIG. 4 Place a sheet of the water/vinegar-soaked paper on a cooling rack sitting on a sheet pan. Arrange the soaked leaves on the paper, shiny-side down.

FIG. 5 Lay a piece of iron water–soaked paper over the leaves. Add a second layer of leaves and repeat, alternating types of paper.

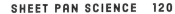

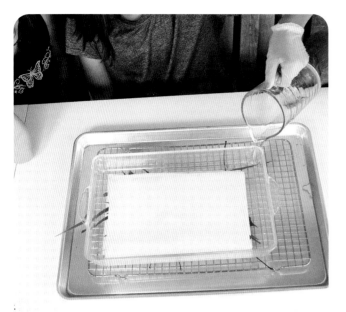

FIG. 6 When stack is complete, weigh it down using a flat-bottomed, heavy dish. Add some water to the bottom of the sheet pan.

FIG. 7 Cover the pan tightly with foil and bake at 350°F (180°C, or gas mark 4) for 30 minutes to steam the paper. Let sit in the oven for another 30 minutes after you turn it off.

FIG. 8 When the pan has cooled to room temperature, remove the foil and pull the stack apart to reveal the eco prints created by the iron in the water and the tannin in the leaves.

ACKNOWLEDGMENTS

Books are a collaborative effort, and I am extremely grateful to the team of talented people who made this book.

First, thank you to the team at Quarry Books: my longtime acquiring editor Jonathan Simcosky, art director Heather Godin, project manager and copy editor Liz Weeks, senior marketing director Angela Corpus, school and library marketing manager Mel Schuit, and the entire design and editing team. I am fortunate to have such a skilled, supportive group to work with.

Thank you to my brilliant, cheerful literary agent, Rhea Lyons.

As always, I am eternally grateful to Minneapolis photographer Amber Procaccini for capturing the science projects and kids so beautifully.

Thank you, Bridget, Cela, Declan, Divya, Django, Finola, Gunnar, Haakon, Julian, Kiran, Lachlan, Liam, Mark, Maura, Raina, Ravi, and Scarlett, for being amazing model scientists.

Finally, thank you to my family and friends—especially my husband Ken, our kids Charlie, May, and Sarah, and our wirehair pointer Heidi, who brings a tennis ball to every photo shoot.

LIZ HEINECKE has loved science since she was old enough to inspect her first butterfly. After working in molecular biology research for ten years and getting her master's degree, she left the lab to kick off a new chapter in her life as a stay-at-home mom. Soon she found herself sharing her love of science with her three kids as they grew from toddlers to teens, journaling their science adventures on her online educational platform KitchenPantryScientist.com.

Her desire to spread her enthusiasm for science led to a career in science communication and writing, with regular TV appearances, speaking engagements, and her books: *Kitchen Science Lab for Kids* (Quarry Books), *Outdoor Science Lab for Kids* (Quarry Books), *STEAM Lab for Kids* (Quarry Books), *Star Wars Maker Lab* (DK), *Kitchen Science Lab for Kids: Edible Edition* (Quarry Books), *The Kitchen Pantry Scientist Chemistry for Kids* (Quarry Books), *The Kitchen Pantry Scientist Biology for Kids* (Quarry Books), *The Kitchen Pantry Scientist Physics for Kids* (Quarry Books), and *Radiant: The Dancer, The Scientist and a Friendship Forged in Light*, an adult nonfiction narrative about Marie Curie and Loie Fuller (Grand Central Publishing).

Most days, you'll find Liz at home in Minnesota, reading, writing, creating science experiments, singing, playing banjo, and following her kids' activities. Liz graduated from Luther College with a bachelor's degree in art and received her master's degree in bacteriology from the University of Wisconsin, Madison.

AMBER PROCACCINI is a commercial and editorial photographer based in Minneapolis. She specializes in photographing kids, babies, food, and travel, and her passion for photography almost equals her passion for finding the perfect taco. Amber met Liz while photographing her first book, *Kitchen Science Lab for Kids*, and she knew they'd make a great team when they bonded over cornichons, pâté, and brie. When Amber isn't photographing eye-rolling tweens or making cheeseburgers look mouthwatering, she and her husband love to travel and enjoy new adventures together.

INDEX

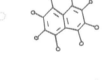

Kitchen Science Lab for Kids

52 Family Friendly Experiments from Around the House

978-1-59253-925-3

STEAM Lab for Kids

52 Creative Hands-On Projects for Exploring Science, Technology, Engineering, Art, and Math

978-1-63159-419-9

Kitchen Science Lab for Kids: Edible Edition

52 Mouth-Watering Recipes and the Everyday Science That Makes Them Taste Amazing

978-1-63159-741-1

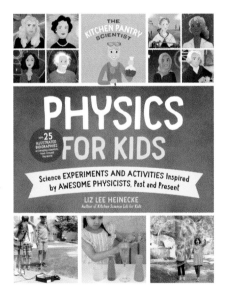

The Kitchen Pantry Scientist Physics for Kids

Science Experiments and Activities Inspired by Awesome Physicists, Past and Present

978-0-7603-7243-2

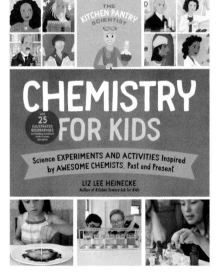

The Kitchen Pantry Scientist Chemistry for Kids

Science Experiments and Activities Inspired by Awesome Chemists, Past and Present

978-1-63159-830-2

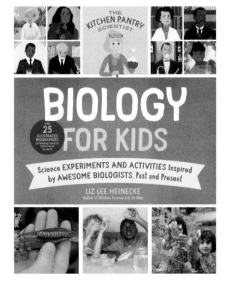

The Kitchen Pantry Scientist Biology for Kids

Science Experiments and Activities Inspired by Awesome Biologists, Past and Present

978-1-63159-832-6